Circles of Stillness

Circles of Stillness

THOUGHTS ON CONTEMPLATIVE PRAYER
FROM THE JULIAN MEETINGS

Edited by
HILARY WAKEMAN

DARTON · LONGMAN + TODD

First published in 2002 by
Darton, Longman and Todd Ltd
1 Spencer Court
140–142 Wandsworth High Street
London SW18 4JJ

ISBN 0-232-52450-X

A catalogue record for this book is available from the British Library.

Designed by Sandie Boccacci
Phototypeset in 9.75/12pt Garamond ITC
by Intype London Ltd
Printed and bound in Great Britain by
The Bath Press, Bath

Contents

SECTION FIVE

'There are many beginnings': life stories *87*

SECTION SIX

'A pain by truth, a bliss by love': Julian and others *103*

SECTION SEVEN

'A well to draw on at need': The Julian Meetings *119*

Foreword

Silence is God's first language

'Silence is an escape,' said my visitor, as if to settle the matter once and for all. 'I couldn't agree more,' I replied, somewhat to her surprise. 'But is there anything wrong in an escape? Did not prisoners in the war escape in their hundreds, and did we not praise them?' 'It was natural,' she said, 'that they should want their freedom.' 'And it is natural that I should want mine,' I replied, 'which is why I keep silence.'

Jesus said, 'You shall know the truth, and the truth shall set you free' (John 8:32). Silence is an escape into truth because in the first place it is an escape into God. Self-knowledge is a fruit of silence. People who know themselves could never speak of others as we commonly read and hear today. 'Condemn not,' says Jesus, 'and you will not be condemned' (Luke 6:37). To the one who knows themself, condemnation of the person, as person, as distinct from the deed, would be the breaking of a tryst with truth. To another it is less serious, being largely a fruit of ignorance.

If one of the fruits of silence is self-knowledge, it must follow that another is humility. Who can know themself and remain proud? Every virtue we may exercise through the day must be shot through with humility if it is to become its true self. Thus without humility, patience is not true patience, goodness is not true goodness, generosity is not true generosity. And so we might go on. Silence before God works to purify every fruit of the Spirit.

The truth sets me free, not of course free to follow every impulse of my impetuous nature but free rather to be the sort of person God wants me to be. Being is more important than doing, not because doing is unimportant but because right doing springs from right being. God is the ground of our being. The silence, of which this book pre-eminently speaks, roots us more firmly in that ground.

Silence helps me to become a complete and whole person. In silence before God we meet the emerging, unfolding and deeper self and in this encounter new energies of the spirit are released. In silence resistances are overcome, prejudices are broken down, passions are subdued, fears are dissolved, memories are healed, relationships are enlarged and a new spirit comes to irradiate our lives which become increasingly marked with trustfulness and thanksgiving. Yet, good though that is, it fails to rise above enlightened self-interest and therefore should not be the prime reason for the keeping of silence. For those called to silence it is one of the love offerings to God we are called to make every day. It is only as we come to see silence in this way that we shall have the resolution to observe it and stay with it daily.

And yet how we try to escape silence! When the time comes for silence a phone call we might have made earlier becomes extraordinarily important. Or the writing of a letter, or a visit to the shops: the list is unending. In one of his retreat addresses, Bede Griffiths tells how the monks of Downside would come to their Abbot and say: 'I feel I'm wasting my time. I sit there and nothing happens and my mind wanders about. I ought to do something.' And the Abbot would always insist: 'Don't "Do something" . . . Sit, and give that half hour to God.' Bede Griffiths comments:

> That is the essence: you take that half hour every day, morning and evening if possible, and you give that half hour to God. If he lets you have wandering thoughts all the time, or if he lets you go to sleep, you accept that, but you try to be open, to surrender to him and allow him to work in you. This is the crucial point: we can prepare ourself, we can have the body and the breath and the mind, but the prayer has to come from God. Contemplation is what we aim at. It is the activity of God, the Holy Spirit in us, it is not ourselves.

'You take that half hour every day,' writes Bede Griffiths.* This raises an important point. If you belong to a Julian Meeting you only take that half hour with the other members every month, or every fortnight, or at the most every week. The spirit of the Julian Meetings is not operative in our lives unless we make every effort to get a time of silence (whatever length of time we fix) at least once every day. I suppose that a solid meal once a fortnight is better than nothing, but our bodies will hardly thrive. Is it so different in the world of

* Bede Griffiths, *The Mystery Beyond* and *On retreat with Bede Griffiths* (Medio media/Arthur James, 1997).

the spirit? And yet how difficult it is to keep this time when we are on our own. Let me say this: it becomes much easier if we have a companion. Happy are those who can find a prayer partner in their own household. But if you can't, and if you live for much of the day alone it should not be difficult to find one or more who would be glad to share for their sake as well as yours. I write here from experience, experience of my own failures when alone, and of the help I receive from others who join me in my home. Donald Nicholl, of beloved memory, once wrote that when two people share a silence they bestow healing upon one another. How true have I found that to be.

We live in a dark and uncertain world. Several years ago I copied out, and have since kept by me, the following words written by the Mother Superior of the Sisters of the Love of God: 'More and more I think the only response to the increasing horrors of what is going on is silence. It is all so dark – but perhaps only in standing in silence in the darkness can I see that tiny light coming into the world and know the ground of my hope.'

Mother Teresa of Calcutta, in 1981, asked members of all faiths to meet our darkness with a daily prayer for peace. We are asked to give one minute to it either vocally or meditatively.

> Lead me from Death to Life, from Falsehood to Truth.
> Lead me from Despair to Hope, from Fear to Trust.
> Lead me from Hate to Love, from War to Peace.
> Let Peace fill our Heart, our World, our Universe.
> Peace Peace Peace

(Announced at St James' Church, Piccadilly, Summer 1981)

But Mother Teresa was an apostle of silence and with such who are likely to read this book she would, I think, have gone further. 'We need silence', she wrote, 'to be able to touch souls. The more we receive in our silent prayer, the more we can give in our active life. God is a friend of silence. The essential thing is not what we say but what God says through us.' The sacrificial offering of silence to God, with such love and devotion as is given us (he asks no more), takes us to the heart of intercession. An intention before our prayer is all that is needed; perhaps not even that as the cause is already on our heart. The pattern of prayer is unchanged. Thoughts and imaginations are allowed to drop away as before, as we let them fall unreflectingly into the arms of God. He works. He knows. He understands. Thoughts and words may so easily get in the way. 'Silence is God's first language,' writes the Cistercian, Thomas Keating, 'everything else is a poor translation.'

Circles of Stillness, edited by Hilary Wakeman, the founder and ongoing encourager of the Julian Meetings, is a follow-on from *Circles of Silence* published in 1994. It draws on writers experienced in silence and the ways of the Spirit and there are some splendid articles and inspirational poems. I recommend this book unreservedly to all who are called, or waiting to be called, to the contemplative life without which no religion, however diligently followed, can do more than touch the surface of our deepest needs.

Robert Llewelyn
October 2001

SECTION ONE

'Enhancing the ordinary, making the extraordinary simple': contemplation

Quotation

EDDIE ASKEW

We are human beings, not human doings.

– One of his opening thoughts at the
1999 Julian Meetings' UK retreat

Vision

JOY FRENCH

Like angels' wings
(Angels themselves unseen)
The heavenly messengers
Pass and repass
My clouded eyes.
What do they bring?
Blessings: the gift of sight.
And take away?
Terrors: the fear of night.
Ah, dearest Lord
Who came to be our Light,
Let me sing praise
Each day, each night.

The garden within

BARBARA MUIR

Nature's response to the Creator does not involve mental activity.

Recently I was talking to a friend trained as a church worker, about the Julian Meetings and silence. 'Oh,' she said, 'I never could see the point of that.' Afterwards it dawned on me that there is no point to it – it is like the seed growing silently and unseen in the dark, and it may not be observed until the leaves are visible; nature's early response to the Creator does not involve mental activity and sound. Dorothy Gurney wrote,

> One is nearer God's heart in a garden
> Than anywhere else on earth

and we may take a leaf from nature's 'book without words' and realise that peace and beauty are not confined to all the colours of the garden, for we have the pilot light of the Holy Spirit within us. If we sit down at a regular time for a regular space, maybe only five minutes at first, after naming to the Lord one by one the burdens, sorrows, irritations that weigh heavy on us, and the blessings, then repeat a word or phrase, e.g., 'Maranatha' ('Come, Lord, come') or, from the Psalms, 'I said to my soul be still and wait for the Lord', we may gradually or suddenly become aware during our daily round that the Holy Spirit is prompting, putting in touch and guiding in another way: those little coincidences have a deeper meaning.

The repetition of a word or phrase ('rather like sucking a sweet', as Robert Llewelyn says) helps to keep stray and persistent thoughts from taking hold of our minds, and frees our hearts to be attentive to the Holy Spirit within. For me, many tries over the years and much perseverance were needed before I ever felt comfortable and 'at home'. It is a precious gift for sharing.

Could it be that, as with nature, a corporate silence would bear fruit beyond our imaginings? Are the flowers in the garden aware of the part each plays in the glory of creation, or of the garden where they grow – and what of their scattered seeds?

The following sentences are from a meditation by Wang Weifan, theologian at Nanjing: 'Without winter, how could we greet the arrival of spring? These are the laws of nature. Are the laws of the Spirit any different?'

Contemplation

IVY BISHOP

Contemplation is round;
Wheels within wheels?
Certainly not a line
Or a train of thought.

Contemplation is movement,
Perhaps a spiral
Going deeper and deeper
Into experience and meaning.

Contemplation is recollection
Of all that has been,
Searching in memory
For forgotten graces.

Contemplation is looking
Beyond the obvious
Towards the mystery
Content to let it be.

Contemplation is assurance
That "All shall be well,"
"For now we see through a glass, darkly
But then face to face."

Moments of contemplative joy

MARY HOLLIDAY

Jesus chose his disciples both to be with him and to be sent out.

Contemplative prayer, taught and practised in the Julian Meetings for the past twenty-one years, is the prayer of silence. It is the prayer of stillness, of waiting, of 'loving regard'. It is the flowering of all our natural senses, set in a framework of silence. Contemplation is seeing, in silent awe, the invisible God. It is hearing, in silent listening, the word from the eternal Word. It is touching the fringe of the garments of the divine. It is tasting quietly the food of perfect Love. It is smelling the noiseless incense of God who is mystery. It is a total feeling of the still presence of the heavenly Lover in a total joy without words. Contemplation is full of wisdom and deep understanding but it is entirely simple. By it we are taken away from the activeness of life without denigration of everyday living. It enhances the ordinary and makes the extraordinary simple. It is a gift from God, never the result of our own efforts. We do, however, need to be open, disposed to the bliss of silent communion with God, allowing ourselves to be inwardly quiet, letting distractions become positive. This prayer, this 'being with God', inwardly gazing in wonder, is received gently and practised without ostentation.

Some have thought the prayer of contemplation is the last rung of a spiritual ladder, reserved for saints. Perhaps it is more like the bottom rung for everyone who takes a small faithful step onto that ladder of perfection. It is also all the rungs in between. So John Dalrymple, in 'Longest Journey', describes seven happenings in contemplative living and reminds us that they do not come in any special order. They are when 'the mind in prayer ceases to follow a process of reasoning'; 'in prayer, words diminish and sometimes stop altogether'; 'thinking diminishes and loving grows'; 'activity in prayer diminishes, passivity grows'; 'intellectual clarity diminishes, bafflement increases'(!); 'consciousness of self diminishes, consciousness of God grows'; and finally 'prayer descends beneath the surface of life and enters the depths of our personality'. Clearly the experiences of the contemplative way are not stages in spiritual progress and there should be no judgement of ourselves or others about where we are. There is no top class of proficiency nor any lowest marks!

Alan Placa, an American Roman Catholic, describes contemplation as 'my personal surrender to the fact that God is contemplating me'. It is therefore essentially a relationship (as all prayer is) – a being with God – a sharing in the life of the Infinite – a resting in God – an alert resting. It is not a prize but sheer gift; it is not something created by us, but a discovery of treasure. The amazing paradox is that we may have, as in the title of a book by Thomas Merton, 'Contemplation in a World of Action'. Because it is deep, precious, given and silent, it is not therefore a selfish withdrawal from the world or a denial of the earthiness of life. It is the finding of a power to cope with life and an experience to make sense of other experiences. It is itself a paradox, a 'dazzling darkness' (Henry Vaughan, 'The Night'), an indescribable joy, a mysterious but 'homely' grace. Thomas Aquinas spoke of the active life and the contemplative life, and also of the apostolic life. This last, he said, was the best of all because in it we 'share with others the fruits of contemplation', which is never an end in itself, for as Unity is inextricably linked with Mission, so is contemplation linked with action. Jesus spent much time apart in order to be able to serve as God's powerful instrument. 'Mount' and 'multitude' experiences are complementary and he chose his disciples both 'to be with him' and to be 'sent out'. Contemplation is so finely tuned that it speaks of perfect balance.

As Julian groups meet, people enter into an amazing heritage – of those who have in the past lived contemplative lives, in the desert, in communities and in the so-called ordinary circumstances of life. We learn from their delightful and often few words describing this prayer, and by being silent together we share their fruits and our own, for all have something to share. With a word, a symbol, or music used to gather us, about half an hour is spent in silence. There is no aspiration to spend long ecstatic hours in the simple act of 'gazing on God'. Of Teresa of Avila it was said that she was never in a state of 'infused' (given) contemplation for more than half an hour at a time. How encouraging for all of us! We may have long times of personal silence in our private prayers, overlapping times of activity, but we may also have brief 'contemplative moments'. An experience reveals a sudden glimpse of God and we see more than is immediately obvious, for contemplation is a special kind of seeing.

My own favourite experience of a contemplative moment was like this: the occasion was the fortieth anniversary of the British Council of Churches, in St Paul's Cathedral. I knew that the Revd Harry Morton, a past Secretary and past President of the Methodist Conference, would be there in spite of having suffered a massive stroke a year or two before. When he was brought into the cathedral in an impressive procession, the late Dr Kenneth Slack, the Director of Christian Aid, was pushing Harry in his wheelchair. As I saw these two men (I had eyes for no others once I had seen them) it was a mystical seeing, for I perceived a personification of caring in the attitude of Kenneth Slack, noticeable in his height, his white hair and his red robes. It was a true pride of the right kind, that he could bring his friend who could not walk with the rest. Harry was beaming . . .

In that brief awareness I was capturing a moment of eternity. Without the words I have used about it since, I was experiencing something of God's limitless love. It is even more remarkable to recall because there was a sequel, proving that it was not only my experience, subjective and imagined, but a moment in which God chose to give revelation to any who had eyes to see. Several years later Dr McArthur was preaching at the memorial service for Kenneth Slack in Westminster Abbey and shook me to the core by recalling the same moment which he described as a sacramental one.

We should treasure these moments and recall them in times of dryness. We learn to develop our spiritual eyesight (insight) by going about with an awareness of things around us, small and great. A contemplative moment may come as we look carefully at a tiny insect or a delicate flower, as we stand in awe watching a sunset or a vast expanse of sea or sky. It may come as we see a face revealing joy or pain or compassion.

Contemplation is not a knowing about God, and may seem like darkness or emptiness. It belongs to waiting – as R.S. Thomas says, 'the meaning is in the waiting' ('Kneeling', from *Collected Poems, 1946-1968*, published by Hart Davis/MacGibbon, 1973). Rather it belongs to 'unknowing'. Words may lead us into wordlessness, sounds may lead us into silence, pictures may lead into prayer without images and people may lead us to communion with God. The needs of the world may lead us to 'contemplative intercession' (Mother Mary Clare SLG), for while we are not groups for intercessory prayer, the contemplation of God may help us to share his own compassion in his own silence with caring rather than requesting.

The Julian Meetings have meant a great deal to me and many

others since they first began. Corners of homes, community chapels and religious houses have been hallowed by simple silent gatherings of exploration into the heart of all praying. Long may the groups continue, for:

> Philosophers know God;
> Christians believe in him;
> Meditative souls consider him;
> But the contemplative possesses him.
>
> (François Malaval, 17th century)

Silence

JUSTIN BARNARD

Inverse of the sound of nothing
this soundless nothing
something awesome
is

lives in eyes that speak
lips that kiss
grass that's whisperless

is
all there was
in that first ethereal Breath
when all was mere imagining

soon to be
birth-pangs of galaxies

but now
no grass
no eyes
no lips
no kiss

Sinking into silence

MARGARET SILF

A word from you, to change my world today.

Coming to stillness in prayer can feel a bit like beachcombing. Walking slowly along the shoreline, simply noticing the movement of the waves and the brush of the breeze on your skin, and all the while alert to whatever treasure may be left at your feet by the tide.

There is sacred space at the meeting point. The waves break over the shore. Waves of my lived reality. Those things that occupy most of my conscious being, most of the time, simply breaking and leaving a shower of spray as a last image of themselves against a steady sky. The waves of my lived life breaking against the bedrock of your truth. And that is prayer, and that is sacred space.

The waves of my prayer are gentle today, just asking for a little space to land and break. There are days when they heave themselves over to you like grey mountains, heavy with pain and the unmanageable forces of their own energy. Sometimes they just come lapping quietly, spreading themselves ever so thinly over the flat sandy beach.

They come under heavy grey skies, reflecting threat and fear. Or they sparkle when the sun shines, and scatter happiness like foam across the rocks. Or they creep in tears to seek your comfort, and linger in the rock pools, begging for shelter until the tide turns.

These are my prayers, Lord. And yours is the rock, and the solid beach and the steady shoreline. And I meet you in this sacred space. You receive me there and I wander in my prayer like a beachcomber. From time to time there are gifts in the shingle. A beautiful shell that reflects the colours of eternity. A persistent crab that raises a family in the rocks, against the odds, against the tide. A word from you, to change my world today.

The moment isn't for ever. The waters of our meeting are soon sucked out to sea again. Drawn back into the swell again, but never the same. The tide of prayer ebbs, and I am back on the high seas. No longer who I was a prayer ago, nor who I will be another prayer away beyond the next tide's turning. There is sadness in withdrawing but there is strength in the power of the swell, and there is hope.

Prayer has happened. Your gift given and received, at the breaking point, when my tide spreads itself in a gesture of surrender and my waves collapse, exhausted, on the shore. Prayer happens when I break into the spray on the bedrock of your reality.

There is a long day ahead, until my tide can flow onto your waiting beaches. And the rock remains, and the beaches. Only the tide moves in and out.

Astonished and amazed

JOYCE RUPP

Like tulips long lying hidden
suddenly springing forth
making beauty out of sunlight

Like soil caught and turned,
warm, moist, and ready for seed,
opening its heart for growing

Like spring speaking to the day
about the goodness of the earth,
patterning green on every plain

Like trickles of raindrops
smoothing earth's rough edges,
healing hardened hillsides

Like all these quiet miracles
so is the coming of Spirit,
telling of the surge of life

Urging me to gaze again
upon my very common days,
to look within and be amazed.

(Acts 2:7)

Quotation

MEISTER ECKHART

There is nothing so much like God as silence.

SECTION TWO

'Through the Cloud of Unknowing': God

Quietude

JOY FRENCH

O, the blessedness of silence!
Time without times,
Without the watch of clocks,
The chatter and whine of radio,
The flashiness of the telly!
Time to become still,
Restless fingers relaxed,
Breathing quiet,
Spirit at peace;
The person personal,
Not diffused, not scattered hither and thither,
Becoming aware
Of self
Of you
Still there:
Still
And here.
Deo Gratias.

Early waking

JOY FRENCH

Time
To winnow the harvest of dreams,
To unravel the chorus of birds;
Time
To uncoil, yawn, stretch,
To re-inhabit the body,
Salute

The stiff hip, the bruised toe
(Old comrade; new acquaintance).
Time
To breathe deep;
To become aware
Of self,
Of You,
Quietly there.
Time to give thanks;
Time
To be.

Imaging God

GRAHAM JOHNSON

The whole of the Bible can be seen as a story of a people continually changing their ideas about what God is like.

In the parable of the talents (Matthew 25:14-30) the servants have different images of their master. When the master returns the first two servants report what they have done and they expect their master to be pleased. The third servant says, 'Master, I knew you to be a hard, demanding man so you can understand why I hid your talent.' The first two servants perceive their master as generous, forgiving and loving: the third as hard, demanding and critical.

This parable confronts us with the rather startling idea that the only God we are able to experience is the God we image. That is an awesome thought. Many people have images of God that are not really of God but a distortion of God. For such people a healthy spiritual life is impossible. It is very important that we be sure that our images of God and God's nature and character are faithful to the gospel.

J.B. Phillips has a list of a whole range of distortions in his book *Your God Is Too Small* (Epworth Press, 1952). He lists differing images that people have of God: a policeman, a grand old man, absolute perfection, a meek and mild character, a heavenly eiderdown, or a managing director, etc. The problem is that once someone has an image of God it is extremely difficult to change it. It has become an engraved, graven, image.

How do you go about changing your image of God? It is a relief to some people to know that they are free to change their image of God. It is good to allow stories about God to change your image.

The parables of Jesus were meant to do just this – would you rather have a generous, loving parent as your God or a harsh, demanding one? In fact the whole of the Bible can be seen as a story of a people continually changing their ideas about what God is like. Now the Spirit continues that work. Stories in modern novels can continue to show us how people change their ideas of God. Here are two examples:

> 'My first step from the old white man was trees. Then air. Then birds. Then other people. But one day when I was sitting quiet and feeling like a motherless child, which I was, it came to me: that feeling of being part of everything, not separate at all. I knew that if I cut a tree my arm would bleed. And I laughed and I cried and I run all around the house. I knew just what it was. In fact when it happen, you can't miss it . . . God love everything you love – and a mess of stuff you don't.'
>
> (Alice Walker, *The Color Purple*,
> Harcourt Brace Jovanovich, 1982)

> 'In my dream God the father, with his great beard and stern expression, yielded to Grandmother, with her keen, shrewd, far-seeing eyes. From now on it would be she, seated in the clouds, who would take care of the world, set up wise and just laws. Now all would be well for the poor people on earth . . . For a long time I was haunted by the idea that it could not possibly be a man that made the world, but perhaps an old woman with extremely capable hands.'
>
> (Gabrielle Roy, *The Road Past Altamont)*

You must be honest with yourself. God must be true to your experience. So often God gives us important experiences in our lives but we miss the meaning. I do not mean visions or things like that. I mean ordinary experiences that can give us some inkling of what God might be like. Being a parent is a good example of this.

When we set aside time for prayer it can be a help to use a

Christian symbol as a particular focus: a candle, cross, star, bread, chalice, wedding ring, water. These suggest images such as living water, bread of life, light of the world, etc. They also help move us on to times when images of God are either taken away from us or are no longer helpful in prayer as we wait on a God beyond images.

'Raise the stone and thou shalt find me'

People have asked about the above quotation, used on some of the Julian Meetings' cards. It is from the hymn by Henry Van Dyke (1852–1933):

> They who tread the path of labour follow where my feet have trod;
> They who work without complaining do the holy will of God;
> Never more thou needest seek Me;
> I am with thee everywhere;
> Raise the stone and thou shalt find Me; cleave the wood and I am there.
>
> Where the many toil together, there I am among my own;
> Where the tired workman sleepeth, there I am with him alone;
> I, the peace that passeth knowledge,
> Dwell amid the daily strife;
> I, the bread of heaven, am broken in the sacrament of life.
>
> Every task, however simple, sets the soul that does it free;
> Every deed of love and mercy done to man is done to Me.
> Nevermore thou needest seek Me;
> I am with thee everywhere;
> Raise the stone and thou shalt find Me; cleave the wood and I am there.

The original words, 'Lift up the stone and there shalt thou find me; cleave the wood and I am there', are from the *Oxyrhyncus Papyri*, edited by B. P. Grenfell and A.S. Hunt (1897), Sayings of our Lord, Logion 5 1:23. This may be the basis of Van Dyke's hymn.

Shrift

JOY FRENCH

Coming again to grace,
After long absence, I recall the way
The winding stair,
The silence and the peace;
And You are there.

Heart pounding, mind in spate,
I kneel, and I am blessed.
My listed sins become irrelevant.
Words falter, but the intent
Is honoured: ah, my Lord!
You do the rest.

The quest for God

MARTIN ISRAEL

The mystic affirms that whatever we say about God is wrong, therefore silence is more eloquent than speech.

Recently an Anglican priest was relieved of his parish after circulating a basically atheistic view of reality. He is a member of a small, but by no means insignificant, group of ministers who deny any God outside the individual's own consciousness, making this God merely the sum total of the person's best thoughts and aspirations. A theology of creation is absent from this account of reality, and any thought of survival of death is dismissed, almost with ridicule: once the brain is dead, that is all there ever will be of the person whose earlier consciousness may have embraced vast tracts of aesthetic, scientific or altruistic endeavour.

It is no wonder that this movement is described as post-Christian; indeed, any relation with basic Christianity seems purely fortuitous apart from moral considerations. These can be found in all the major world religions as well as in many aspiring people who have long had the integrity to call themselves atheists, inasmuch as the God of theistic religion so often seems to be either vicious or incompetent. There is not a little in the early Old Testament to substantiate the former view, while the intolerable calamities that punctuate human history would point to divine carelessness if not frank cruelty. It is not easy to justify a contructive divine existence on a purely intellectual consideration.

But God is not known primarily with the reason. There is an even more powerful place of recognition, which is called traditionally the soul – the point of a person's true identity. In the immortal words of *The Cloud of Unknowing*, 'By love may he be gotten and holden, by thought never.'

The unknown writer of this English classic was, like his or her near contemporary Julian of Norwich, a great mystic. A mystic is one who seems to have been granted a direct awareness of the divine presence so that they are filled with the divine light of illumination as well as the divine heat of love. Such a person is inwardly changed, and by his or her very presence brings hope and understanding to those around them who are open to a new view of reality.

'By their fruits you shall know them' is a perfect canon of judgement. Reading the works of the great mystics fills any sensitive person with a joy of recognition that leaps out of the darkness of worldly agnosticism and lights up the way with love, joy and peace. What was always known in the depths of the soul is now confirmed in the life of the person, who can then proceed with hope and love. It would seem that the direct awareness of the God who transcends all human understanding lights up the divine spark within all humans so that they may proceed in the darkness of intellectual doubt to the light of a new day where loving concern will work in concert with enlightened reason. The end is a growing wisdom that inspires the whole world with a dynamic concept of God in all things as a reflection of the God beyond all names, whose essence is best expressed in purely negative terms.

Where does the brain come into all this? It is the organ that receives all information whether sensory, physical or spiritual (by which I mean the awareness of the divine in the moment at hand), and is able to process each piece of information into an intelligible unit of intelligible communication. In this way we cease to be merely inspired individuals, but become units in a mass of humanity, conferring our insights and gaining new understanding from those around us. The problem of the body-mind relationship remains a perennial point of debate, with at present the non-dualists like the radical clergy mentioned at the start of this article holding sway. To them the mind and soul are merely particular cerebral functions. Artificial intelligence in avant-garde computers would seem to substantiate this monistic view.

The classical Cartesian dualistic view sees body and soul as two separate functions of the person, both working in the closest unity through the agency of the brain while the person is alive, but also capable of various degrees of dissociation especially in very psychic types of people. At physical death the dissociation is final and complete according to this point of view, one held without any difficulty by both psychic people and mystics, who are spontaneously aware of the transcendent God, sometimes called the Godhead, by whom we can appreciate the immanent God in the 'apex of the soul', commonly called the spirit in mystical language.

Nobody with physiological understanding would deny the paramount importance of the brain itself while we are alive in the flesh; the debate is where its psychical and spiritual information originates. The atheist would cite the brain as the place of origin, whereas the spiritual person would see the place as far off in terms of human understanding.

It is extremely doubtful whether someone devoid of this transcendental vision is capable of being a minister of religion in any of the world's great faiths. This of course does not imply that the essentially atheistic view is wrong, but if it is indeed true, all religion and its worship will be progressively dismissed as pathetic superstition, and the world will become even more heartless than it now is: nothing will be of enduring value, and the wise man will be the one who takes the material advantage of the moment with little concern for anyone else. At present this type of person is considered anti-social, or even criminal. But if there is no transcendental reality and no survival of bodily death, does anything matter except our own immediate advantage? Wisdom will consist in fooling as many people as possible in our selfish quest for the things of this world.

God is indeed a mystery. The mystic affirms that whatever we say about God is wrong, therefore silence is more eloquent than speech. When we do our daily task as selflessly as possible, we will never be far from the divine source radiating its goodness into our very being. As we give to others, so the unknown God gives of himself/herself to us, and we move progressively into the divine glory.

A poem from Cape Town

BETTY MITCHELL

You are Lord:
O may all my being
Sing your sovereignty.
May it sing from,
And of, within,
And with, and to
The Wonder
Of Your ever-present,
Ever-radiant
Love and power,
Your all-sustaining essence,
Which human words
Cannot describe –
Yet dares
To adore.

The meaning of things

BASIL HUME

> *Each visitor to Cardinal Basil Hume's lying-in-state at Westminster Cathedral Hall in 1999 was given a small memento – a card with Cardinal Hume's photo and this brief but relevant extract from his book* The Mystery of the Incarnation (*Darton, Longman & Todd, 1999*).

The meaning of things, and their purpose, is in part now hidden but shall in the end become clear. The choice is between the Mystery and the absurd.

To embrace the Mystery is to discover the real. It is to walk towards the light, to glimpse the morning star, to catch sight from time to time of what is truly real. It is no more than a flicker of light through the cloud of unknowing, a fitful ray of light that is a messenger from the sun which is hidden from your gaze. You see the light but not the sun.

When you set yourself to look more closely, you will begin to see some sense in the darkness that surrounds you. Your eyes will pick out the shape of things and persons around you. You will begin to see in them the presence of the One who gives them meaning and purpose, and that it is He who is the explanation of them all.

A meditation on the Trinity: a poem derived from Psalms 19 and 29

DAVID SPURLING

Day cries of this to silent day:
silent night to night.
Silent light transforms the earth again.

God sees in me;
God feels in me,

Yahweh makes me new.

Day cries of this to silent day:
silent night to night.

God sees with me;
God walks with me;
Jesus makes me new.

Day cries of this to silent day:
silent night to night.

God works through me;
God burns through me;
Spirit makes me new.

Yahweh's voice in splendour makes us be;

Spirit over countless waters speaks us free;

Whisperings of my heart
Are echoes of his truth.

Day cries of this to silent day:
silent night to night.
Silent light transforms the earth again.

SECTION THREE

'The ultimate letting go': the work of prayer

What do we really mean by silence?

WANDA NASH

> *Where there is an absence of words, we are exposed to a space that can be extraordinarily threatening.*

It is strange how easily we who are happy with praying in stillness can take our own understanding of it for granted. We can become too familiar with absolute basics. Is it possible to be too comfortable with silence?

The National Retreat Association mounted its millennium conference at Swanwick. It was called 'Crossing Thresholds'. One of the thresholds for me was a challenge to re-examine what silence really is. I was conscious of opportunities to use silence in small blocks and large blocks, in plenary meetings as well as in intimate groups, in worship and in passing personal conversations. As I watched all of these droplets of what, to me, was living water, I found some surprises.

It is too easy to assume that silence is felt as a safe place. For many, silence feels very unsafe. Where there is an absence of words, we are exposed to a space that can be extraordinarily threatening. All the scaffolding of everyday support falls away – and what is left? Sometimes there are images that take over. That might be all right if I can choose my own images, but what if images that I can't control intrude, and those that I don't want persist? Things I have been carefully blanking out with noise – when the noise goes there they are with all their terror. Imposed silence can be violent.

So why should I choose to go into silence? Do I think it is to hear God? But how do I know it is God speaking, and not my own fantasies and longings being projected into the silence?

Do I go in as part of a search for peace and quiet? Could it be a ploy to get away from the things that bother me, the demands being made on me? To others, this escape into silence can be a powerful act of withdrawal, even of rejection. They may think I want to absent myself from them.

Do I use silence as a way of living out the tenet, 'If you can't say something nice, say nothing at all'? That sort of silence can mask my hostility, or resentment, or jealousy, or confusion. An absence of response is not always felt by others to be full of peace; it can seem judgemental, showing an unwillingness to be open or communicative. It can kill interaction with others.

Do I rely on silence to protect myself? When I don't feel brave enough to speak out against things I see as being unjust or uncivil or unkind, I can just keep quiet and place myself within the silent majority. This is the ruse that allows awful things to happen simply by leaving them unopposed.

So why do I spend most of my professional life and a considerable amount of my private life developing the spaces in silence? How can I be sure of the difference between what could be called unconstructive silence and that which truly brings me – and others – closer to the divine Godhead and his purposes for the world?

Sometimes I think that going into silence is simply an opt-out; but however it is used, silence is powerful. This awareness is paramount. It puts the choice onto me. I can choose to play the power games that are noted above, to the detriment of others. Or I may choose to face my complete powerlessness before God, something I must acknowledge before the power of God can begin to pour through me.

It must surely be truer of the use of silence than almost everything else that 'by its fruits you shall know'. Does the silence I choose add to the yearning and love for God in this here-and-now, as far as I can discern it, or does it diminish it? Does it add to the humility and trust and abandonment that I feel Jesus Christ is seeking from me, or does it add to my sense of spiritual arrogance and superiority? Does it enable me to pray more for the needs of the world or less?

Always, and all ways I know, I must be aware of other people's experience of my silence as much as my own. And that means never becoming too familiar or too comfortable about it, but holding it tenderly enfolded in mystery and wonder – as Dame Julian has taught us.

In light inaccessible

CHRISTOPHER GREGOROWSKI

The test of our praying is not in our feelings but in our daily lives and relationships.

A companion I have turned to often over many years is *The Cloud of Unknowing* by that dear, witty, sage and down-to-earth old 'Anon'. I say 'old' only because he lived so long ago. His personality and mine differ in one important respect: I have not been able to follow him, St John of the Cross or Thomas Green into the valley of desolation. Nor do I give myself to the work of contemplation as completely as he demands. And I am far more active than he would like me to be. Yet I find myself rereading him and invoking daily the sentence which has become my aim in praying: 'Lift up your heart to God with humble love: and mean God himself, and not what you can get out of him' (Chapter 3).

'Anon' suggests that we use a word of one syllable – 'Lord', 'Christ', 'God', 'Love' – which we may ask the Holy Spirit to supply each day. We say this word repeatedly and slowly, with our breathing in and breathing out, while we lift up our heart to God with humble love. We receive 'Lord', 'Christ', 'God', 'Love' as we breathe in. We worship 'Lord', 'Christ', 'God', 'Love' as we breathe out.

Why do we do this? Because our goal is union with God. Because we are placing ourselves in God's hands and asking him to be at work within us, to do with us and make of us whatever he wills. St Paul, having shared with us Moses' secret about the fading glory, gives us the basis of contemplative prayer in the final verses of 2 Corinthians 3: 'Now the Lord is the Spirit, and where the Spirit of the Lord is, there is freedom. And we all, with unveiled face, beholding the glory of the Lord, are being changed into his likeness from one degree of glory to another; for this comes from the Lord, who is the Spirit.'

Being changed into his glory is not a matter of acquiring a halo that can be covered in a paper bag and revealed when it is removed. God is love, and to share his glory is to be filled with his love, and to love as he loves. God is fully revealed to us in Jesus Christ, the divine Son made fully human, and to share his glory is to become mature human beings.

The acid test of our praying is not in our feelings while we are at prayer but in our daily lives and relationships. The short question is: Am I more loving because I pray? Do I love God more? Do I love others more? Do I love myself more?

This is God's call to us, and God can enable us to answer his call only if we are willing to 'strike that thick cloud of unknowing with the sharp dart of longing love, and on no account whatever think of giving up.'

I close with the words of a hymn that expresses who God is and why he is hidden from our eyes:

> Immortal, invisible, God only wise,
> In light inaccessible, hid from our eyes . . .
> All laud we would render: O help us to see
> 'Tis only the splendour of light hideth thee.

Christian Zen

GILLEAN RUSSELL

> *Letting go over and over again produces a new awareness of dependence on the Source of Life.*

We were exchanging a first and last word at the end of a Christian Zen retreat. Some were familiar with Zen, but for most of us it had been a very new experience, physically and spiritually, for we had been 'sitting' for six hours a day under the watchful eye of a Zen 'Roshi' (who is also a Jesuit priest).

Zen is not a religion, although it is usually associated with Buddhist practice; it is a way of experience cut off from dogma and philosophy. We were shown how to sit in as near the lotus position as we could manage – the neophytes were immediately apparent as we struggled to arrange ourselves in a position that we could hold without moving for twenty-five minutes at a time!

With Zen it is the practice that is important. We were given a basic instruction on the 'how' and left to our own experience. 'What' and 'Why' were not our concern. Words like meditating and contemplating were not used, we were simply 'sitting'. In order to stop the mind running on ahead or delving into the memory bank we were advised to be aware of our breathing, no more than the reality that all we can do is to let go of our breath and the in-breath follows and it is beyond our control to stop it. The gift of life comes with each breath and all we have to do is to surrender our breath and wait to be filled. We may know that, but focusing on the letting go every minute over and over again produces a new awareness of dependence on the Source of Life. It implies a letting go of the non-essentials, a simplification of prayer style and life style. For one often struggling with contemplative prayer it gradually opened up a way to let go of the thinking process and discursive activity.

So much apophatic experience produced in me a new longing for God and a great appreciation of liturgy. The evening mass each day was an oasis of quiet activity and met the longing. Zen outside this framework would have been a desert I would have found hard to cope with. I also realised how much I needed the community of those who were in the retreat with me. I do not believe that I could sustain twelve periods a day of stillness and silence were it not for the sake of the others. If one person had fidgeted it would have broken something for the whole group. We lack this discipline in our teaching now, training is so valuable when the going is hard. We do not value enough the holding that our praying community should provide.

Apart from being aware of our breathing the only suggestion that was made to help us focus was the use of a word (not called a mantra) of a single syllable, such as is suggested in *The Cloud of Unknowing* – 'God' or 'Love' which could be repeated silently on the out-breath.

I suppose in time I shall be able to say that the position in which we sat was a 'prop', but I shall have to wait until my hips are more accustomed to being turned inside out! The body, when poised in the lotus position is balanced and it does not require great muscular effort to hold the position. That has a message for my daily life as well.

The retreat was led by Fr Gebbard Kohler SJ, who is German and lives in Japan but comes to Europe regularly to give retreats. He relates Zen to the writings in *The Cloud of Unknowing*, and his daily talks were an inspiration for anyone searching for the contemplative way.

Eloquent silence

MARTIN ISRAEL

> *In the depth of silence we may experience a new awareness of ourselves, one no longer circumscribed by our own character with its preferences, prejudices and envy of others . . .*

The paradox of silence is that of being the medium of profound communication. In the flow of normal conversation we tend quite unconsciously to exclude much of what others are saying, registering what is of importance to us personally and rapidly forgetting the rest. The more rapid the interchange of ideas, the less accuracy we may achieve in assimilating what is being said; the more heated the exchange, the less we may understand its contents. Eventually the sheer noise of the verbal exchange may deafen us into silence, no less emotionally than physically. At last we can relax in wordless, noiseless quiet.

The practice of silence is the basis of meditation. The mind is evacuated of all thoughts but retains its alertness, otherwise it could easily relax into sleep, excellent as this state of consciousness is for the body's maintenance day by day. Of what is one aware in the silence of meditation? The nothing that is everything, the void that is the basis of all that exists. What we know intellectually and feel emotionally is the outer form of the tangible world; what we experience in meditation is the essence of all that exists. It both precedes and defines all forms, yet is itself beyond rational description. This foundation of reality is one way of referring to God, who is in fact beyond finite description and yet closer to us than our own body. It is for this reason that the more we think, the further we retreat from God. 'By love may he be gotten and holden, but by thought never', we read in *The Cloud of Unknowing*, that glorious mediaeval English mystical treatise. It is a sad paradox that formal religious practice can soon expel the Spirit of God, especially if it is verbose or contentious. Those presiding rapidly assume the function of the Deity themselves!

In the depth of silence we may experience a new awareness of ourselves, one no longer circumscribed by our own character with its preferences, prejudices and envy of others who seem to be more successful in the world's eyes than we are. A stillness overshadows when we can be truly quiet and know the consoling love of God's presence in the way directed by Psalm 46:10-11. This loving silence is the heart of prayer. It asks no questions, makes no demands, but simply flows out in amazed thankfulness at the undemanding limitlessness of the grace of God. Prayer is silent communion with God, sometimes known as a personal presence and on other occasions as the transpersonal source of creation whose identity is universal. God loves us as people not only because we are special in his sight but also as individual creatures with a preordained plan to perform. It is in the eloquent silence of attention that we may learn the nature of this work and the means of fulfilling it. Jesus reminds us not to be anxious about food and drink to keep us alive and about clothes to cover our body. Surely life is more than food, the body more than clothes. Look at the birds in the sky; they do not sow and reap and store in barns, yet our heavenly Father feeds them. Are we not worth more than the birds (Matthew 6:25-6)? The superiority of humans over the animal and vegetable orders lies in their mental power and aspiring moral concern, that goodness should prevail over evil actions and attitudes. But the adverse side of intellectual brilliance and moral superiority is the tendency to use the mind for self-enhancing, even destructive purposes, as has been evidenced by the development and proliferation of lethal weapons of war in the twentieth century culminating in nuclear energy. Even moral concern may develop into a pernicious tendency to take control over other people's lives. This inclination is not unknown in the practice of orthodox religion. 'Good' people can be decidedly trying companions! The way to curb these adverse aspects is humility. This is not acquired by the power of the will so much as through life's rich tapestry. We learn about our own weaknesses by experiencing the disapproval of those close to us; by divine grace these defects of character are healed, and we are encompassed by an aura of humility. This is the trustworthy way to silence, at first to contemplate our own weaknesses in honest appraisal. As the process continues, so it is imbued with love in the presence of which we know the grace of God. Thought is transcended by love which flows out as a mighty stream, at first for those we know but ultimately for everyone, friend and enemy alike.

Prayer may be considered in terms of the practice of loving silence in which the ego is abandoned. We will not merely do our own work, admirable as this may be, but become completely open to God's will. This is so indescribable that we proceed with the trust of a little child. This is the essence of faith, which is the other component of prayer. It is indeed the core of the cloud of unknowing.

Prayer in the body

HEBE WELBOURN

> *A Hebrew word* nephesh *occurs frequently in the Psalms and is variously translated throat, neck, desires, spirit, life.*

Martin Israel, in his talks at a Julian Meetings' retreat, referred to the head or the intellect as the centre for meditation; the head, as it were, being the head of the hierarchy of the body. He spoke of placing one's awareness within the head and perhaps visualising a cross between the eyes. I have heard this described as looking from within the cross which was placed upon my forehead at baptism. Martin Israel also referred to awareness centred in the heart and in the solar plexus.

In pre-scientific times one's anatomy was experienced from within. Now we tend to think of our brains, heart, liver, etc., as being featured in a chart or model in a schoolroom. Oriental tradition described our pre-scientific anatomy in terms of centres of energy, or chakras. There could be five chakras within the body: brow, throat, heart, solar plexus, and sacrum or womb. In addition, just above the heart and the base contact with the ground could be thought of as crown and root, making seven centres in all. Contemplative awareness could be centred in one or other of the chakras, but wholeness was associated with the flow of energy. Another aspect of bodily awareness lay in the aura, a kind of energy-field surrounding a person. When I use the Celtic Cairn prayer (as in 'St Patrick's Breastplate' and Richard Adams' book about it, *The Cry of the Deer*, Triangle, 1987) I seem to experience a kind of energy field round me – something like an aura.

There are many ways in which this kind of awareness can be helpful in Christian contemplative prayer. Anthony de Mello has some suggestions. Ancient Orthodox tradition associated with the 'Jesus Prayer' included breathing exercises similar to yoga, in which the prayer was directed down into the heart. Instruction included a warning not to descend below the heart into the belly or sexual regions! As a woman, I have found that some of my most profound, creative experiences seem to be centred in my womb, and in any case it is impossible to ignore a part of me which has been so much part of daily existence. The warning, however, is salutary. We need to travel in company with others who can guide us on our way.

My own guidance has come from various sources apart from those mentioned above. Firm in my own conviction that it is Jesus Christ I am in love with – not the Buddha, etc. – I have taken part in Buddhist and yoga meditation exercises. To describe some of my own physical awareness experiences:

The brow – sitting behind my baptism cross. My unconscious mind extends in the presence of God into infinity. The background colour is purple light.

The throat – sometimes choked by tears. Yearning. All my desires. Singing. Speaking with tongues (not that I personally do this; I'm more for silence or perhaps singing, myself). A Hebrew word *nephesh* occurs frequently in the Psalms and is variously translated throat, neck, desires, spirit, life.

The heart – the experience of sap flowing after long sorrow (Hildegard of Bingen's 'greening'). Love centred in the breasts. Arms for giving, serving, receiving and embracing. Sitting centred in compassionate suffering. Blue light – one of Mary's colours.

The solar plexus – Martin Israel described this so well. Gut fear. Fight or flight. 'Butterflies in the stomach'. Jealousy. The bilious humours of the liver in alchemic tradition. Yellow. Coming to prayer vulnerable, anxious, even terrified; full of unresolved resentments and anger. Sitting in sultry sulphurous yellow until it is transformed to gold. Gradually finding myself enabled to use the energy of my fears.

The sacrum or womb – depth of feeling. The recognition of feelings related to sexuality and excretion. Orange/red/black: the earth colours of the early iconography of Mary. Prayer expressed in the poetry of the Song of Songs. For me, wisdom is experienced as a quickening somewhere deep within me. It is also, in a real sense, 'down to earth'.

Some people, reading what I have written, will find sparks of recognition. To some it will seem fanciful or even distasteful. However it may be, our silence must be physically earthed.

Being - and doing

EDDIE ASKEW

> *You can't keep love under glass like a specimen butterfly impaled on a pin of piety.*

Sometimes, I'm tempted to sit back and say to the Lord, with the exaggerated politeness I tend to use when I'm actually very impatient, 'Lord, can you please make up your mind? In your own time, of course, but can you tell me simply, and clearly, exactly what you want me to do?'

You see, I've been reading two books. One, *The Way of the Heart* (DLT, 1981), describes the spirituality of the early Desert Fathers that came from long solitude and deep meditation. It emphasises the importance of being, not doing. For me, it underlines our present lack of time for prayer. The second is Michel Quoist's *With Open Heart*. He's an activist. 'God,' writes Quoist, 'isn't going to ask, What did you dream? What did you think? What did you plan? What did you preach? He's going to ask, What did you do?'

So it's not enough to be, you've got to do! And we all know the lack of time for that. The easiest thing may be to stop reading and thinking and just react to circumstances. Some do. But when you go a bit deeper things start to get clearer. The desert solitude wasn't a cop-out from the world, but a recognition of the need to have something good to offer the world – real insight, a deep awareness of God's loving nature – experiences which are found in the quiet, with God. Quoist starts at the other end of the same line and reminds me that personal Christian experience has to be turned into action. You can't keep love under glass like a specimen butterfly impaled on a pin of piety.

There's a balance needed but, being a balance, it's delicate, and we tend to overweight things one way or the other depending on temperament. Some of us rush around doing, some are quietly being, and we all wish the others were different! It's interesting to read Philippians 3. Paul tells us who he was – a Hebrew, a Pharisee; and what he'd done – zealous in work for his faith, obedient to the Law. In his new life being and doing are combined again. All he cares for is to know Christ – being – but then to press on towards the goal, putting what he knows into practice – doing (Philippians 3:14). We try for the same balance, aware, I hope, of our own bias to one side or the other, and understanding the bias of others.

Lord, the trouble is
I want it all cut and dried.
A clear path set out for me,
an easy set of instructions,
a route map I can't possibly misinterpret.
And what would I call it?
The Lazyman's Guide to the Kingdom?
And you the courier,
helping with the luggage,
moving smoothly from one hotel to the next.
Taking care of all the problems.
Life one long holiday.

You expect more of me than that, Lord.
You show me a real world of choices,
questions I have to face, decisions to make,
tensions I must learn to balance
as I move along the road.

I need the quiet times with you.
The times when we can sort out our relationship,
just you and me.
When we can concentrate on who and what I am.
But who and what I am only become real
back in the world outside.
You were the Christ throughout your life,
but without the focus of the cross
your purpose would be blurred, half done,
and that's not done at all.

But doing needs a centre point
to give stability and strength.
A starting place, from which the purpose comes.
So one's no use without the other.
The building needs foundations.

And I begin to see my hopes for what they are.
Child's dreams of life, clear cut,
though not so innocent, and feather-cushioned from reality.
Served up, well cooked, on a warm plate.
Life's tougher than that.
The choices must be made,
and with each choice
the risk of right or wrong.
The tensions stay, but so do you.
To share it with me.

I am content.
No, that's not true,
I'm not,
But I'll settle for uncertainty,
with you.

I remember, I remember

DAVID CONNER

At a profound level we human beings co-inhere, are part of each other . . .

From what people say, it seems as if almost all experience which is claimed as 'religious' contains, to a lesser or greater degree, some enjoyment or anticipation of a state of harmony, reconciliation and unity. It is as if the deeper the religious experience, the greater is the sense of the apparent distinctions and contradictions of this world being overcome. Without denying the enhancement of our awareness of ourselves as personal beings, so much talk of God tends towards God's 'oneness'; God as the source and goal of unity. It indicates that God's effect upon this world is always to bring about deeper coherence. You can see why it is that it is so natural to attribute to God the quality of love, since love, above all, engenders and expresses union.

In our times of prayer we co-operate with some deep-down

impulse – the Holy Spirit – towards a final union. In that yearning which is at the heart of prayer; in that reaching out and in that lifting up of our hearts we begin to taste something of the oneness of our destiny; we begin also to thirst for that destiny more urgently.

When we pray, however, we do not do so as separate and isolated individuals. Each of us is part of an intricate system of relationships and, at a profound level, we human beings co-inhere, are part of each other, always bearing each other on our hearts and in our minds. Everyone who prays is a kind of representative and all prayer is a kind of intercession. Whenever we hanker after God we carry others with us willy-nilly; we bring others into God's presence.

The prayer of intercession as we usually understand it involves us in the deliberate making conscious of that fact. That 'making conscious' is our 'remembering' of those people who are already, because they are part of us, offered in each prayer that we might utter. Memory is that which most sharply serves to draw others towards us and, through us, to God. Our rememberings are God's gifts to us as God equips us to be God's fellow-workers in the drawing of this world towards its destiny.

Such an understanding of the significance of memory sheds light upon the importance of all our ordinary memories. Each and every remembering is itself a prayer. The people we remember on birthdays and anniversaries; friends called to mind almost accidentally by surprising jolts and associations; the living and departed whom we remember as ones to whom we owe some debt of gratitude; all these are, in the ordinary run of events, caught up in our lives and, in so far as our lives are God directed, drawn close to God. The cultivation of memory can indeed be a great service to the world in which we live. A routine birthday card or thank-you note might carry more weight than we generally imagine.

Perhaps even more mysterious might be the fact that in every remembering we share in the mind of God. Quite recently the Archbishop of York was reported in *The Times* as saying, as he reflected on the 'biology of the soul', that an individual's identity was 'held in the mind of God'. Our personal continuity, this or the other side of death, depends on God's remembering. It might just be that the 'remembering God' uses above all our memories in the 'holding in being' of all that has been created and of all that is destined for unity with God.

The human memory might be a powerful extension of the

sustaining and sanctifying energy of God as God seeks to draw this all-too-fragmented universe into some intimate harmony and union. Maybe those lists of people to send cards to on their birthdays and at Christmas time, and all those fleeting memories brought to mind when reading newspapers or watching television or simply day-dreaming are, far from the distractions that we sometimes feel them to be, darts of spiritual energy which we would do well to value.

Prayer everyday - an approach to prayer

JOHN WILSON

> *Inner peace is not freedom from the storm, but calm amidst the storm.*

We are all travellers on a spiritual journey that leads to God.
Prayer Everyday provides a path which can be followed at will by the contemplative traveller.
The rate at which we travel along the route is decided by the traveller not by the designer of the road.
The stages in the journey can provide a way of progress in prayer for eight weeks, or eight months, or for a year or more, depending on where the travellers start and how quickly they want to travel.
Like a favourite walk, the route, or parts of it, can be returned to quite often when we want reassurance.

On seeking inner peace

Most of us would benefit greatly if we could find a time and a place to seek personal peace each day. Amid the seriousness and turbulence of each day it is still possible to find a sense of inner calm. We all have so much to do in this world of care and worries that we have little time to seek and find peace. However, much happiness can be gained by anyone who decides to give time each day to seeking and finding inner peace. This can be done in our homes and places of work as well as in our churches and places of worship. Peace thus found will grow within us and spread to the people we meet, bringing quiet and calm wherever we are. Inner peace is not freedom from the storm, but calm amidst the storm.

Everyday link: When we recognise a stress situation or relationship in daily life, we recall the feeling of inner peace. We let it help us to behave or react calmly.

On seeking the peace of Jesus

Having developed the habit of seeking inner peace, we reach a point where we want or need to have a clearer image in mind than the general idea of peace and a sense of calm. As Christians we all have one person we can focus our attention on to help us. Irrespective of denomination or preference, Jesus is the one person we can believe in and listen to. He said, 'Peace be with you', and, 'My peace I give you. My peace I leave with you.' When seeking inner peace we now have someone to guide us. Jesus is our friend and guide.

Everyday link: When we recognise a stress situation or relationship in daily life, recall the peace of Jesus. Let it help us to behave or react calmly.

Prayer of Word and Prayer of Thought

We started by seeking inner peace and we have moved on to thinking about the peace of Jesus. As we do this, a feeling of love and respect starts to grow – love for Jesus and respect for others.

When we think about the love that Jesus showed – caring for, curing and helping people before dying to save us all – we want to thank him. We want to thank him for all he has done for us and all he has given to us. When we pray, we think of God with love. We thank him for his love which continues to this day and beyond – "I will be with you until the consummation of the world." We introduce Prayer of Thought as well as Prayer of Word when we consider the sheer enormity of God's love for us.

Everyday link: When we recognise a stress situation or relationship, recall how Jesus was able to help people. We ask Jesus for help to behave or react calmly.

Reading and listening

From seeking inner peace we moved to thinking about the peace of Jesus and we have started to consider his goodness. We try to respond to it in word, thought and action. We now move on to reading scripture as a means of listening to Jesus to find out more about him. The Old Testament contains the scriptures that Jesus knew and used in his teachings. The New Testament tells us about him, what he did and what he taught. Like the Israelites of the Old Testament, the Christians of the New Testament and of today are the Chosen People of God. Careful reading of the Scriptures (do not try to read too much too soon) gives us a clear picture of how we should live as active followers of Jesus. Being chosen means that more is expected of us. We have been given gifts. We must use them.

Everyday link: When we recognise a stress situation or relationship, recall what we have read about Jesus curing and forgiving people. 'Forgive us as we forgive others.'

The quality of prayer is measured by the quality of life. Greater peace. Greater humility. Greater love and respect.

Prayer as a means of keeping hope alive

SHIRLEY RAWLINS

> *How can a teapot pour out a cup of tea before being filled with water?*

> They're wounded for the want
> of being listened to;
> they cry
> and too few hear;
> they slowly die
> and too few mourn.

These lines, from Kate Compston's poem 'Seeds of Hope' (previously printed in the *Julian Meetings Magazine* and then in the book *Circles of Silence,* ed. Robert Llewelyn, Darton, Longman & Todd Ltd, 1994) express the deep hurt felt by those who long to speak of things that are important to them but have no one to really listen – and there are many of them. We are all so wrapped up in our own plans and schemes that we cannot spare the time to listen to our own hearts, let alone the hearts of others. We need to take time to listen to the stories, dreams and thoughts of those who have no voice, but, as the poem says, through these who spend time to listen

> a healing comes
> and there are seeds of hope.
> There is tomorrow
> germinating in today.

This healing comes through those who pray, who listen to God in their own hearts, in the world of people and of nature and who use the gift of listening to help those who are wounded for the want of being listened to.

Silent, listening prayer is a means of keeping hope alive; as well as bringing hope to others. It sustains our hope and brings healing and peace in our own souls. The seeds of hope germinate best in listening to God. God is our sure and solid hope, the foundation of everything that is and that we are. God is the source and strength of all we do. If this is so, how can we not listen to him? If we do not, we are going to live lives of fragmentation, disunity and disharmony. The seeds of tomorrow can only germinate today if we listen.

We need to listen to God as St Paul says, by 'praying at all times'. This does not mean that we are to be thinking of God every moment or saying words to him all the time, but through a discipline of prayer our hearts become attuned to him as an instrument is tuned to play the notes of music correctly.

We need to develop a relationship of love with God in our own prayer that keeps our hearts fixed on him even when we are not physically praying. So prayer is a relationship; it is much more than words, more than thoughts, more than images or concepts, it is a deep silent resting in God, allowing him to quieten our minds so that we can listen with attention and be aware of his presence and guidance in our daily tasks.

As we spend time in silence we gradually develop a relationship with God as we would with a friend. Relationship starts with acquaintanceship where we meet a person and exchange pleasantries but little more. It can end there or it can develop into friendliness where we might go out of our way to meet this new friend but we do not have any depth of conversation with them. If this relationship is to go any further it must deepen and grow. We will want to spend more and more time with this friend, and as we do, the relationship can go on to develop into intimacy where we will be able to share our deepest secrets with that person in a trust that says, 'I know that you will not treat my feelings lightly, that however silly I may seem at times I can trust you to take me seriously, and that you will listen to what I am and what I have to say unconditionally as indeed I will with you.' This is the sort of relationship we need to develop with God. To develop such a relationship of trust and affection it is no good if we chatter away all the time – it will become a very one-sided affair and very self-centred on our part. We must listen to what our new friend has to say as well if it is to be a truly shared friendship.

Our relationship with God, which Jesus has made possible through his obedience, death and resurrection, is, however, the very best of relationships because he gives us so much more than we could ever dream of asking for. His unconditional love, generosity, forgiveness and healing are spontaneous and continuous when we respond with love in prayer. How can we be of any use or help to another person if we are not first filled with the love of God? How can a teapot pour out a cup of tea before being filled with water? This filling with the love of God comes through our relationship in prayer, especially prayer that is listening prayer, where the Holy Spirit prays in us 'with groans too deep for words'. This is the prayer that Jesus prayed when he 'went out alone a long while before day.' It was the vital well of stillness upon which he could draw to enable him to carry out his ministry. This is the reality of our prayer, meeting the tenderly loving gaze of God resting upon us. This is the spring of living water that wells up and leads to eternal life that Jesus promises to all who ask.

Learning to pray this way demands a discipline, regular times of silent prayer when we probably feel we are wasting time, with maybe a sense of the absence of God. But as Julian of Norwich says,

> often our trust is not complete, because of our unworthiness and because we are feeling nothing at all; for often we are as barren and dry after our prayers as we were before . . . (but) our Lord is most glad and joyful because of our prayer; and he expects it, and he wants to have it, for with his grace it makes us like to himself in condition as we are in nature, and such is

> his blessed will. For he says "Pray wholeheartedly, though it seems to you that this has no savour for you; still it is profitable enough, though you may not feel that. Pray wholeheartedly though you may feel nothing, though you may see nothing, yea, though you think that you could not, for in dryness and in barrenness, in sickness and in weakness, then is your prayer most pleasing to me, though you think it almost tasteless to you. And so is all your living prayer in my sight."

As Julian says, our trust is poor and not complete, so our prayer seems dry to us.

If we set time to be apart with God every day, even though it is dry and tasteless, the fruit of prayer will be a growing awareness of a new dimension to life. We will build up a reservoir of silence upon which to draw throughout each day as the need arises. There will come an acquired taste for silence, an ability to let go of unhelpful emotions and other harmful influences. A new understanding of how to love unconditionally, and seeing the fundamental goodness in others. There will be an openness to giving and receiving. There will be an enrichment of our ordinary prayer life and a greater clarity concerning our motivation in life. As we grow in our relationship with God, there will be a genuine hearing of the cries of the poor.

This hearing of the cries of the poor takes us back to the poem: 'they cry and too few hear.' Listening to God in prayer helps us to hear God in those cries. The poor may be our closest neighbour but we have been too busy to hear. A favourite quotation of mine is from *Middlemarch* by George Eliot. Dorothea says, 'There is so much suffering in the world. I think of it as a muffled cry the other side of silence.' Listening, silent contemplative prayer is a way to learn to know God and to allow him to be all he wants to be in us, and then we will do the things he wants us to do and let go of what we think is important and trust him.

So let us 'pray without ceasing' by listening to God, to ourselves and to others. Let our listening, silent prayer be a reservoir of love. As we practise silence we can help to channel our prayer in three ways as recommended and practised by Gonville Ffrench Beytagh, former Dean of Johannesburg: first by looking and listening to the things around us, then by longing (or, as Julian of Norwich would say, yearning), and finally by loving. The author of *The Cloud of Unknowing* said, 'By loving he can be gotten and holden, by thinking never.' So let us try to slow down our thinking and learn to love in silent, listening attention. Our intention to pray is all that is required as we let go and become still before the loving gaze of God.

Jesus said, 'When you pray . . . go to your room and close the door, and pray to your Father who is unseen. And your Father, who sees what you do in private, will reward you' (Matthew 6:6). This room is not a room in a house, but the inner room of our being. We are the temple of the Holy Spirit, and as such, our inner room is that place where no one but God can enter.

To summarise these thoughts then, our prayer is the expression of our faith and hope, our response to the love of God. As we let go of our own desires and thoughts we wait in silent receptive trust for God's love to give us the power to be channels for his love to others as we do his will in the world. So, we hope, we respond, we pray and we serve with humility and patience, but with an ever greater desire to love and to become more like Jesus every day.

On self knowledge

SIMON GOODRICH

> *Lighten our darkness we beseech thee, O Lord.*

I listened to a sermon recently, in which the clergyman preached on the Pauline doctrine that we fight not against men, but against the principalities, the powers of darkness. It struck me then how much more explicit is the Eastern teaching on this matter. The astanga yoga, the eightfold yoga, describes its first two stages as *yama niyama*, the 'restraints and observances'. These very closely reflect our Christian doctrine of the vices and virtues. In yogic thought the cultivation of virtue and the rejection of vice are seen as the essential foundation upon which the contemplative life is based. Parallel to this, however, runs the teaching that in order to attain contemplation, the hindrances to this, the *klesas*, must be seen and overcome. The *klesas* are described as egoism, aggression, depression, a clinging to the physical life; and the fundamental source of all these is *avidya*: blindness, ignorance or nonseeing. This is a very important principle, because it sees *avidya*, spiritual blindness, as a first cause, coming before sin and vice themselves. The practice of meditation, or contemplative prayer, becomes therefore the means by which we see our way out of the maze. Implicit in this teaching is the belief that if we could clearly see the fruits of our actions, the personal unhappiness to which these acts assuredly lead, we would abstain from sin.

The interest of this yogic teaching is that in its essence it reflects the often misunderstood Christian doctrine. The word 'sin', in the Greek from which it is taken, is *hamartia*, translating as 'aim' or 'direction'. We sin because our aim is wrong, we head in the wrong direction. If, again, we could clearly see the place to which this road leads, the final, rather than the initial repercussions of action based upon vice, none of us would commit these acts. Our goal, similar to that of the yogic teaching, is not to cease from sin, as of itself this may lead only to a repression or a postponement of our true desires. This is a strong statement, but the much publicised downfall of some of the television evangelists in America highlights the danger of this path. Our true goal is to dispel the spiritual blindness out of which these acts come. This in essence describes the difference between the 'contemplative' and the 'religious' approach. We do not seek to repress or deny our own desires, but to develop levels of insight in which we can distinguish between that which is transitory and impermanent, and that which is eternal. 'Lighten our darkness we beseech thee, O Lord.' For in dispelling our blindness, in coming to see where each road leads, we are no longer tempted to sin.

Learning about the Jesus Prayer

RACHEL KEARY

A prayer that began in New Testament times.

On a cold day last October I attended a prayer school dealing with the Jesus Prayer, led by Martyn Hope from Christ Church, Heathmont. The Jesus Prayer, 'Lord Jesus Christ, Son of God, have mercy on me a sinner', has a very long history and the story of its development is complex. It began in New Testament times, was used and developed by the desert fathers and the monks of St Catherine's in Sinai and, later, Mount Athos in Greece. From there its use spread through the Orthodox Church in Greece and Russia and so to our own time. It is worth looking at something of the significance of the different parts of the prayer.

'Lord Jesus Christ . . .' If the use of our name is important to us, then the use of God's name carries much greater significance. God's name, as revealed to Moses in the burning bush, is 'I am who I am' or the Hebrew 'Yahweh' meaning 'He who is' or 'He who will be'. 'Yahweh' became a sacred name spoken only by the priests and then '*Adonai*' or 'Lord' came into common usage. The Old Testament has many instances of the use of the name of the Lord. The Psalms abound with the uses of the name 'Lord God' as a refuge, a power that comes to our aid, an object of worship. Micah 4:5 contains 'we will walk in the name of the Lord our God'. Peter's sermon shows the use of 'Lord' when referring to Jesus after resurrection, 'Therefore let the entire house of Israel know with certainty that God has made him both Lord and Messiah, this Jesus whom you crucified' (Acts 2:36). The middle name of the title, 'Jesus', was a fairly common name in the Israel of Jesus' time and still is quite common in some countries and cultures. 'Christ' is the Greek translation of the Hebrew 'Messiah' meaning 'the anointed one'. This was originally applied to the anointing of kings and meant 'chosen by God to save people'. The crucifixion and resurrection changes this understanding of who Jesus is. He is God's Son and so is spoken of as Lord in the same way that God the Father is Lord. 'Lord Jesus Christ' shows Jesus as both God (Lord) and a human chosen by God (Christ).

' . . . Son of God . . .' This additional title serves as an explanation of the origins of 'Lord' and 'Christ'.

' . . . have mercy on me a sinner . . .' These last words of the Jesus Prayer bring us personally into the prayer and at first sight could seem a problem for those of us who have poured guilt and negativity upon ourselves. We need to look much further in trying to understand the real richness of this prayer. This part of the prayer is rooted in the Gospels. Two blind men in Matthew 9:27 cry, 'Son of David, have mercy on us.' The publican in Luke 18:13 makes his request, 'God, have mercy on me a sinner.' 'Have mercy' can be as simple as alms giving or can refer to 'reconciliation', 'propitiation' or can involve the idea of redemption. The word 'sin' comes from a Greek word meaning 'missing the mark'. Thus a sinner is someone who 'misses the mark', that is, fails to live as the Lord Jesus Christ would have us live. 'Have mercy on me a sinner' may mean, 'give me your help as without your help I cannot live as you want me to live', or it could mean, 'forgive me for I have failed to do the right thing'.

The Jesus Prayer is a prayer of profound meaning that can keep our 'intent' in mind during silent prayer in the same way as the use of a single word can. It links the Divine with the human and personal and, when used with the reverence deserved, touches our lives in many ways.

Exploring the Jesus Prayer

TAKEN FROM NOTES PROVIDED BY JIM WELLINGTON

> *The Jesus Prayer is often suggested as a mantra or sacred phrase to be repeated over and over again as an aid to moving into the prayer of silence. Jim Wellington says that the Jesus Prayer needs to be approached in its own context.*

The Jesus Prayer – 'Lord Jesus Christ, Son of God, have mercy on me' – can only be properly understood from within the Orthodox spiritual tradition which stresses deification or apotheosis – 'God became man so that man might become God through grace and participation.' Seraphim of Sarov said, 'The object of the Christian life is acquisition of the Holy Spirit.'

The origins of the Jesus Prayer are obscure. Some think that it may have begun in the New Testament Church, others with the Desert Fathers. The first written evidence is in the seventh century but it was very much alive before this in the spirituality of Egypt and Palestine and then, in the Middle Ages, at Athos. It is found in the *Philokalia* (Love of Beauty) which is a collection of the ascetical writing of the Eastern Fathers from the fourth to the fourteenth centuries. In this country the nineteenth-century work *The Way of the Pilgrim* (Anon, tr. R. M. French, Triangle, 1995) has contributed to its popularity.

Prayer of Renewal

It is Prayer of the Heart: Bartimaeus cries out constantly with all his longing, 'Jesus, Son of David, have mercy on me' (Mark 10:47). The Greek word *eleison* means much more than forgiveness. It speaks of pity, compassion and anointing (with the Spirit) to make a person whole (and the Jesus Prayer is part of a whole way of life). It is the cry of those who acclaim the return of a conquering hero. The people call out 'Mercy', meaning 'Give us your riches, let us have our share.' The Christian cries out for the riches of the Spirit, especially love.

It is Prayer of Persistence: as in the parable of the unjust judge (Luke 18:7) or Paul's 'Pray without ceasing' (1 Thessalonians 5:17). It becomes a continual remembrance of God. It takes over your whole personality. John Klimakos says, 'May the remembrance of Jesus be united with your breathing.' He is not talking about bodily techniques. He means part of your whole living, your very life breath.

It is Prayer of Invocation of the Holy Name: Jesus says, 'If in my name you ask me for anything, I will do it' (John 14:14). This sets it apart from the mantra. In the mantra the words are secondary, just a tool to help you into the silence. In the Jesus Prayer the words are crucial. They are a sacramental act making Jesus present. Kallistos Ware called his book on the Jesus Prayer *The Power of the Name* (Marshall Pickering, 1989) and the Fathers saw it as part of an inner warfare, a weapon. John Klimakos says, 'Whip your enemies with the name of Jesus for there is no weapon more powerful in heaven or on earth.' Philotheus of Sinai said, 'Slaughter all the enemies of the land through the unceasing prayer of Jesus Christ.'

It is Prayer of Dependence: it is a work of grace, a rediscovery of baptismal grace. It is not a method into stillness, not a mechanical operation though we do co-operate with God. The Fathers say, 'It can in no way be achieved solely by this natural method of descent into the heart by way of breathing or by seclusion in a quiet and dimly lit place. This can never be!'

It is Prayer of Penitence: the Pharisee and the tax collector (Luke 18:13): 'God be merciful to me, a sinner.' Some add the words 'a sinner' to the Jesus Prayer but this was not used by the early Fathers. Nevertheless it does emphasise an essential element in renewal: repentance, compunction, gift of tears or sorrow for sin. Abba Philemon said, 'But if when you set out on the path of renunciation there is no sorrow in your heart, no spiritual tears . . . no true stillness or persistent prayer . . . then you are still attached to the world and your intellect cannot be pure when you pray.'

It is Prayer of Healing: even though the therapeutic metaphor is less prominent than the military it is present and speaks of the disunity of the human person, through the Fall, being restored through the Jesus Prayer, reuniting the heart and mind, drawing the intellect into the heart. It is part of God's therapy to make us integrated personalities.

Prayer of stillness

Hesychia: The goal of the contemplative life is stillness and union with God, stillness in God. 'Be still and know' (Psalm 46:10). The root of the word 'hesychia' means being seated or concentrated – free from distractions of thoughts (even good thoughts). Philotheos of Sinai said, 'Through the remembrance of Jesus Christ concentrate your scattered intellect.' Gregory of Sinai said, 'Be it even an image of Christ or of an angel or of some saint, or you imagine you see a light in your intellect and give it a specific form, you should never entertain it.'

Nipsis (watchfulness): 'Be sober, be vigilant' (1 Peter 5:8) – keep watch, look out for enemies. The Jesus Prayer needs to be coupled with intense watchfulness. 'Watchfulness is a continuing fixing and halting of thought at the entrance of the heart.' Stillness and union with God is impossible without watchfulness.

Apatheia: detachment from the passions – their control rather than their destruction. By passion is meant something that the soul experiences passively, such as appetite, impulse, desire or feeling, which dominates it. 'Dispassion is established through the remembrance of God'. The remembrance of God was synonymous with the saying of the Jesus Prayer, the fruit of which is the 'warmth of the heart which scorifies the passions.' Stillness and union with God are impossible without apatheia.

Technique: the importance of technique is played down by some of the Fathers. The prayer itself rather than technique brings fruits. It is not how you say it but actually saying it that matters. Nevertheless you can still see monks today following the technique outlined by Gregory of Sinai:

> Sitting from dawn on a seat about nine inches high, compel your intellect to descend from your head into your heart, and

> retain it there. Keeping your head forcibly bent downwards, and suffering acute pain in your chest, shoulders and neck, persevere in repeating noetically or in your soul "Lord Jesus Christ, have mercy." Then . . . let the intellect concentrate on the second half of the prayer and repeat the words, "Son of God, have mercy." You must say this half over and over again and not out of laziness constantly change the words. For plants which are frequently transplanted do not put down roots . . . Restraining your breathing as much as possible and enclosing your intellect in your heart, invoke the Lord Jesus continuously and diligently and you will swiftly consume and rebuke (the evil thoughts), flaying them invisibly with the divine name.

Reflections on revisiting

ANN RICHARDS

> *We can revisit the places which bring us to life and where we can continue to grow. We can go in our imagination.*

The students in the yoga class are lying on the floor. Towards the end of the relaxation time, the tutor asks them to be aware of the side to which they would automatically turn to get up and then to turn to the opposite side 'to make it a new experience'. In the practice of yoga, this is helpful, the student becomes aware of the difference between doing something out of habit and doing it in a different way.

Some decisions in life may seem like this. Do I do what I have always done before (it is safe and may not require much effort) or do I go for something new, take a risk and be adventurous? Perhaps the contrast between these options is not as great as might first appear. There are times when repeating something may be risky. For example, that holiday in France last year was so wonderful that I do not want to risk going again in case it is a disaster this time!

Of course, it is unrealistic to think that we can actually repeat a good experience but perhaps what we can do is to revisit the places which bring us to life and where we can continue to grow. Returning to a place where we have been on retreat can remind us of what was originally so good. We can re-immerse ourselves in whatever it was that was so strengthening and allow time for reflection on the way in which it has affected us.

'Re-visiting' does not necessarily mean a physical movement, we can go to places in our imagination if we choose and sometimes we find ourselves there without any conscious thought. Or again, literature can be revisited. The nature of the written word is such that a book which is reread or a poem which is heard again can seem different the second and subsequent times.

In the case of the Bible, we naturally return to passages which comfort or challenge us and in any cycle of set readings which we may follow, we will hear again verses which are not unfamiliar. Perhaps, either of our own accord or at the suggestion of a spiritual guide, we pray from the Scriptures and consciously use the Bible to listen to what God is saying to us. It could be by *Lectio Divina* ('divine reading') as St Benedict would describe it, or by imaginative contemplation when we put ourselves into a particular story or parable.

It is tempting to think that once we have 'done' a particular passage, our time would be better spent 'doing' another! However, in praying a passage again, different words may stand out or we may meet God in a more profound way.

So . . . do we revisit places or continually search for new experiences? Perhaps the 'or' could be 'and'!

Contemplative intercession

HEBE WELBOURN

> *When we realise that intercession is an exercise in awareness, it brings a great change to our understanding of it.*

JM prayer is, of course, based on silence. After the silence some groups have intercessions. During the intercessions we ask, often in some verbal detail, on behalf of people and causes who are dear to us. At the end of the recent retreat at Park Place, my neighbour turned to me and said, 'I am a newcomer, is JM intercession always like this? I go to my Lydia Group when I want to pray this way. I came here hoping for silent prayer.' I was glad she said this because I was also feeling uncomfortable. I am always uncomfortable with 'shopping lists' of what we want God to do for us. 'Lydia' prayer, at its best, is different – there is openness for the Spirit to provide words. It can happen in any prayer-filled situation that words arise spontaneously. But what about silent, contemplative intercession?

We always come to prayer with our desires. When people came to Jesus for healing, he would look at them and say, 'What do you want me to do?' 'What is your heart's desire?' Desire and beseeching – the first step. As we continue in loving presence we may find our desires subtly changing – 'purifying the ground of our beseeching', in the language of Julian of Norwich. I may also find that my desires are overtaken by yearning on behalf of someone else. And so intercession leads to giving, receiving and sacrifice.

Our yearnings may be quite inarticulate. Lancelot Andrewes wrote, 'More is done by groaning than by words. To this end Christ groaned, for to give us an example of groaning.' We are told that 'the Spirit intercedes for us in groaning that cannot be uttered' (Romans 8:26). Our intercession is part of the divine, inarticulate cosmic groan. Tears, too. We do not often shed tears at Julian Meetings, but intercession is incomplete without them. And just 'sitting appalled' like Ezra when he discovered that the dedicated rebuilders of Jerusalem were indulging in all kinds of corrupt practices (Ezra 9:4). This is no outpouring of emotion, it is just sitting with the pain for as long as may be.

Sitting with the pain can also be a kind of burden-sharing. If we are closely identified with someone or some people in suffering, maybe we can share their burden. Mary by the cross. To see a loved one suffer can be worse than suffering oneself. We never suffer alone. For me, this is often night prayer – like Gail Ballinger's poem elsewhere in this book. I lie insomniac, transfixed with a pain in my soul. Or, maybe, I'm stuck with some kind of physical pain. 'Welded into oneness with Christ's constant interceding' . . . until 'night streams softly into silence.' She describes the experience so well.

Intercession can be like sitting at the bedside of a sick person. I can't do anything but the important thing is that I am there, present. The prayer of presence. Charles de Foucauld present in his hermitage and his followers present in the city among the homeless and the drug-dependent. John Taylor has a beautiful chapter on prayer in his book *The Christ-like God*. He describes how a little girl in a Ugandan village would call on him, sit quietly for a while and then leave saying, 'I have finished seeing you.' So can we, in the same simplicity, just be present in God's presence. If there are friends who creep in with me among my anxious preoccupations, or distracting presences like noisy traffic or emergency services, then these, too, come into the presence of God. Then as we sit, silently present, our awareness of and anxiety for our friends may fade away into a more intense awareness of God's presence.

Watching and waiting is another aspect of contemplative prayer. Watching: alert and yet restfully poised so that we will not tire. Vigilant, attentive, ready for anything. Like a sentry on duty, or a shepherd at night – or a birdwatcher. Watching by a sickbed, watching over the development of a child, watching my partner or lover, watching, like a prophet, the signs of the times. Waiting, waiting infinitely patiently. Softly, slowly. Allied to this is 'spreading it out before the Lord.' Like King Hezekiah who received a letter of final threatening demand from the besieging Assyrian army which he took to the temple and 'spread it out before the Lord,' remaining with it in prayer until nightfall. In that letter Hezekiah spread out the fear of his city (2 Kings 19:14). In the same way we can spread out our fear, anxiety, anger, resentment, guilt, refusal to forgive or be forgiven – and wait for release.

We can pray contemplatively in the zone of spiritual welfare. 'Being peace' is a Buddhist practice, the title of a lovely book by Thich Nhat Hanh. And a Christian practice, too. Not a withdrawal into a cosy, holy refuge – but holding to Peace in the eye of the storm. Attentive to Christ our centre while the dualities and misunderstandings fight it out. Being reconciliation, in Christ, our centre. Being human, we will need to be out there, actively engaged. But to watch and pray is to remain constantly attentive to the Centre.

When we realise that intercession is an exercise in awareness, it brings a great change to our understanding of it. We no longer think in terms of whether it 'works' by bending God's will or manipulating other people's lives. We are not concerned here with our spiritual or psychic powers, not even with our powers harnessed to God's love. Not with intellectual or manipulative powers – not with power games of any kind. The place for all that is out there, in the world of activity.

In contemplative intercession we let go of all power and just wait attentively on our Centre.

Playfulness and prayer

WANDA NASH

> *It is only as I strip myself of my pretensions that the bit of the image of God that is in me is uncovered.*

Playfulness is about abandoning my own concerns into the inventiveness and unexpectedness of another. It's the ultimate let-go: letting go my self-imposed pompousness; letting go my disguised self-pity; letting go of my need to worry and be anxious; letting go of my have-tos, my ought-tos and musts; letting go of my earnestness, my 'worthiness', my trying-hard; letting go of my childishness, look-at-me-ness, tantrums at not-getting-what-I-want; getting free from the relentless tirade of self-criticism. As Richard Holloway in his book *Dancing on the Edge* (HarperCollins, 1997), says, it is 'the real faith of the Christian that is more like a rolling jazz session than a march on the barrack square.'

All this can be undeniably difficult: there has been so much in my education about gaining control, and particularly self-control. About not letting on where it hurts, keeping cool in a crisis, and – being British – about keeping the lid down even when I am exultant. Yet Harry Williams writes that it is only when I am able to

> laugh at myself that I accept myself, and when I laugh at other people in genuine mirth that I accept them. Self-acceptance in laughter is the very opposite of self-accusation or pride. For in the laughter I accept myself not because I'm some sort of super-person, but precisely because I'm not. There is nothing funny about a super-person. There is everything funny about a man who thinks he is. In laughing at my own claims to importance or regard I receive myself in a sort of loving forgiveness which is an echo of God's forgiveness of me. In much

> conventional contrition there is a selfishness and pride which are scarcely hidden. In our desperate self-concern we blame ourselves for not being the super-person we think we really are. But in laughter we sit light to ourselves. That is why laughter is the purest form of our response to God . . . For to sit light to yourself is true humility. Pride cannot rise to levity. (*Tensions*, Mitchell Beazley, 1976)

It's quite simple: playfulness is the antidote to taking myself too seriously. When I feel the approach of that morass of self-decomposition, that threat of being sucked under in the mire of my own insufficiency and ineptitude and blockages (which is in fact the awareness of the sin of the world of which I am a part), it is in turning to the playfulness of the Christ-child that I am retrieved from moroseness. The indulgent depression of self-castigation is never modelled in the Good News. It is only as I strip myself of my pretensions that the bit of the image of God that is in me is uncovered. Whether that bit of his image in me becomes tarnished over the years, or scarred, or distorted or dented, the Creator still delights in it, still wants it to respond by receiving and sharing his delight.

The mediaeval court jester could say things, and spell out truths, that were disallowed and denied in normal conversation; clowns who appear clumsy and awkward and childlike can get away with social protests and ridiculous propositions that we don't ordinarily want to look at. The clown undercuts our so-called intellectualism, and shows up our pomposity for what it is. The clown reveals the preposterous expectations that I cling on to, and allows them to melt away. St Paul claimed that he was a fool for the sake of Jesus Christ, and he would heartily endorse the modern clown ministry headed up by Roly Bain. 'Holy Fools' live out the vulnerability and openness that enable us to glimpse new truth about ourselves and God. Roly Bain insists that holiness and humour go hand in hand. It's about being true to the unique self, and yet not taking it too seriously. To know yourself and yet laugh at yourself. To be able to open up to the daringly unpredictable, and not mind too much how often you get things wrong. That is why children with their insatiable questioning and their unguarded loving give adults the licence to play. He has written in *Fools Rush In – a call to Christian clowning* (Marshall Pickering, 1993): 'Prayer is to be lived and revelled in, rather than said nicely. Maybe too often we end up saying our prayers rather than praying, clinging to the wreckage of dull custom rather than sailing off into uncharted waters.'

Abandoned prayer is marked by its sense of expectancy, readiness for anything, comic, routine, or tragic, but it is without any sort of demand. Real prayer doesn't even assume preferential treatment. It doesn't state its preferred objectives. It says, 'I don't know what is in store for me, but whatever it is I know you will stay beside me as long as I stay beside you.'

Reflections on reflecting

YVONNE WALKER

> *For me the root of religion must be about human experience: what else is the incarnation about?*

I read with delight the article in a recent JM magazine about children spending time sitting round a candle reflecting, focusing and sharing something important from their day (Julie McGuiness, 'When the Children Want to Stop', Section 9). I had just finished six weeks accompanying some very busy people on their journey through Lent, and 'praying the day' is something which many of them have found helpful (see the end of this article for the process). Unlike the children, these people with busy, responsible jobs do not have the luxury of setting aside time to sit with a candle, but often use their morning commuter train journey for a few moments' pause to look back over the previous day with God. The homeward-bound journey at the end of the day was not such a good time – reflecting soon turned to snoozing!

Praying the day can be done at any time, looking back at whatever period of time suits you best. The regular recalling of God's presence in all our experience brings an awareness, an openness and a time to enjoy simply being with God. It may come quite naturally when things are going well, but on the dark days when everything goes wrong, just a smile or a word of comfort reminds us that God is just as much there in the pain and frustration with us. It also shows us how important are the little gestures, a smile, a word of appreciation, a shared cup of coffee snatched in a busy schedule. These mean a lot when reflecting on a stressful, hectic day and remind us that in relationships with others, the little ordinary things can demonstrate how much God loves and cares for us.

Certain comments at the end of Julie McGuiness' article raise important questions for me personally. 'Such emphasis on the experiential approach implies that at root religion is about human experience . . . it ignores the vital issue of the truth claims inherent in different beliefs.' For me the root of religion must be about human experience, what else is the incarnation about? It does not ignore the 'truth claims', it lives them. The God in whom we live and move and have our being invites us to be – to be accepted as the unique creature who is being created, gifted, loved and enfolded by God. Reflecting back and praying the day enables us to be and to live the reality which is the Creed. This and our religious beliefs are not something separate from the deepest experience of being loved and owned by God. The Creed is to be lived and experienced in daily life, not just something to be repeated each week in church, and praying the day is one way to do it.

Here then is how we 'pray the day'; looking back and handing over:

> 'God examine me and know my heart, probe me and know my thoughts.' (Psalm 139)

- Take time to relax . . . ask for the help of the Holy Spirit so that everything in you may be open to God.
- Ask God to show you how he has been involved in every aspect of your life today. Imagine yourself safe and held at rest, 'like a child in its mother's arms', looking back over the day with God, as if you are watching a video replay of the day.
- Allow the moments and events which you enjoyed to emerge, savour them. Tell God how you feel about them.
- Let the day 'play back' again and observe the things you regret. Express your feelings about them to God.
- Now look forward to tomorrow and be aware of the things that worry you. Ask God for what you need.
- Entrust yourself, all that is you, into the tender and loving care of God as you go to sleep. 'God provides for his beloved even as they sleep' (Psalm 127:2).

SECTION FOUR

'A passion and a purpose beyond knowing': difficulties and darkness

A distraction

ANONYMOUS

We sat there in the silence . . . and this noise began to intrude.
Opening my eyes I saw that my neighbour had her glasses in her hand and she was clicking the arms against each other.
The sound totally distracted me.
I longed to lean across and remove the glasses or hold her hand still.
But how could I!

And then I realised what I *could* do – so I prayed.
I prayed with all my heart that this person might, in the silence, find the peace of God;
that the Spirit might flood into her and calm her restless spirit with its presence;
that Christ might be with her in her need;
that the stillness of our meeting might seep into her mind and body and soul.

My heartfelt prayer certainly distracted me from the noise, which stopped after a while.

I was so thankful that God had shown me how to react –
particularly later when I found that the woman concerned was suffering from a form of schizophrenia and felt church people were persecuting her.
I hope and pray that our silence, and my prayers, were of some little help to her in her need.

Silence

CHRIS EYDEN

Excuses for not spending time in silence are a natural protection mechanism against encounter with the unknown.

I am a very noisy person. I love noise. I seek noise for excitement, for stimulus, for information, for company, I rejoice in music and talking, the exchange of ideas and the creativity which I always associate with the communication of God to his world. However, I am aware that human beings can communicate with each other without words, without noise, and without visible activity of any kind. Intuition, perhaps even telepathy, the communication of intense emotion, like love or anxiety, between people who are physically apart are fairly well documented. I therefore conclude that God communicates with us, and we with God, in a noiseless way which we call silence.

When I look at the life of Jesus I find that he spent most of his time living with noise: the noise of the synagogue, the noise of the crowd, the noise of parties and of markets and camels, and towards the end of his life, the terrifying noise of the mob. But at the most significant points in his ministry he seemed to seek solitude. He prayed in the wilderness and was tempted in the wilderness. The isolation of Gethsemane, although inflicted by disciples too exhausted to stand the pace, was a painful and self-revealing experience, pouring out his anguish at his impending crucifixion, to a God whose answer was silence. If Jesus is to be the example for our own lives, then it is clear that a mixture of expansive and communicative engagement and silence before God is necessary for a balanced life of prayer and Christian discipleship.

I hear many instructions and ideas of how we might find silence, like making ourselves still through what sound like New Age yogic exercises in order that we can achieve a blank mind. I must be honest and say I don't find these helpful. I don't believe there is such a thing as a 'blank mind', but what there can be is a more receptive mind, where silence is not so frightening. What silence does is to allow thoughts and feelings, anguish and expectation to rise from the subconscious to the conscious mind. This operates at many different levels, from the relatively mundane to the deeply spiritual or disturbing depths of the psyche. I suspect that it is for this reason that silence makes many people agitated. The number of excuses for not spending time in silence are a natural protection mechanism against encounter with the unknown. I have often been of the opinion that the level of resistance to an activity is a direct indicator of the importance of addressing it.

My misgivings about the Church's renewed call to prayer and contemplation lie in its current almost unfailing ability to tame and domesticate great spiritual and philosophical truths. So the depths of contemplative prayer, as practised by the great spiritual mothers and fathers of the Church, become nothing more than a nice diversion from a busy life. Most of the time it would be more effective and more honest for our middle-class anxiety to be relieved by Prozac or some other tranquilliser. The encounter with silence borne witness to by the great pray-ers of Christian history – names like St John of the Cross, Julian of Norwich, John Wesley, Teresa of Avila, Thomas Merton and others – was first an encounter with the self in all its painful complexity, and then an encounter with God, often in crucified form. Here there is no escape from reality, but rather a greater engagement with it. Praying through silence, then, can carry with it some painful consequences, because 'silence is listening to the truth of things'.

We can be in no doubt that we are at times called to silent prayer, to shut up and listen, to let go of our ideas, however clever, and simply 'be'. Talk can often distort us, words do break bones and do hurt, both ourselves and others. Talk can often surround us like an intricate piece of play-acting, protecting the hearer from exposing our lies and encountering the real self. St Ignatius Loyola wrote, 'It is better to keep silence and to be, than to talk and not to be'. He attributed silence to God; in silence there is no condemnation; in silence there is no aggressive direction; in silence we are allowed to grow and be created. He commended this as a pattern of leadership for the Church when he said, 'A bishop is most like God when he is silent'.

Silence is not trendy. It isn't chic. And it runs contrary to the materialistic and go-get culture which we all live in. To be silent is to some extent to protest. Silence isolates us from the crowds. The society in which we live loves its dissatisfaction and misery because at root it is ill-at-ease with itself and an unhappy civilisation is always loud.

To pray in silence is to encounter God, and the way to pray in silence is to be silent, to take the risk, to find the time, to do and to experience. The activity of focusing the mind is a discipline necessary to all those of us who engage in perpetual busyness. Silence at the beginning of the day leaves the first word, that which activates, to God. Silence at the end of the day leaves the last word and conclusive activity to God.

I think it is unlikely that many of us will become great praying mystics. But it can only be to the benefit of both the Church and the world if many of us shut up and listen. We can only be at ease with God if we are at ease with ourselves sufficiently to be at ease with others. Jung sent a student into a room with the command, 'Lock the door and remain alone in silence for two hours.' After half an hour the student returned anxious and disquieted. Jung's only remark was this, 'If you cannot spend two hours with yourself, imagine what it must be like for others who must spend a lifetime with you.' Prayer to God can sometimes only come out of silence. When all has been said and all has been done, sometimes all that is left is to say and do nothing, waiting. If silence is not much preached today, maybe it is for prayer to preach it. If we don't listen we won't come to any truth, either of ourselves or of God. If we don't pray we won't even get as far as listening. The four things go together: silence, listening, prayer and truth. The Church over the centuries has done a good job of making God rather noisy and difficult, maybe silence is the only scrap of undefiled Christianity that we still have left.

Papering over the cracks

YVONNE WALKER

The need for cracks and gaps is evident all around us.
It allows us space – space to grow – to expand – to move on.
The chick cracks open the shell in order to grow.
The chrysalis is split from end to end to allow the butterfly to emerge.

The clickety click of the train was made by expansion gaps in the track.
Civil engineering depends on gap technology.
We need cracks and spaces to allow for movement and growth
So that we can emerge in a new shape,
Our vision expanded – our horizons extended –
A new me can emerge from the crack.
The very crack which may appear to be a sign of imperfection
But in reality it provides new life – new horizons – a new being –
The next stage – a step forward – don't paper over the crack –
Work your way through it – to a new life.

Searching to escape from the prison of a one-sided rationalistic experience of God

MARTIN HEYNS

(Part of Dr Martin Heyns' address at the JM Annual Meeting in South Africa)

My background as a South African Calvinist makes my contribution on the subject of contemplative or meditative interaction with God, a very modest one. I have no special revelation on silent prayer. Actually I'm only in the process of trying to escape from what I call my one-sided rationalistic perceptions and experiences of God, something I was saturated in from my childhood in the tradition of the Dutch Reformed Church. Therefore at this point and time in comparison with your experience I am perhaps asking more questions and have less answers on this subject.

To start, in my tradition it is fundamental that I live in the faith that I am always in the presence of God. Not only in the theoretical sense of the word. Not because God is in everything and therefore everywhere. It is only through faith that I know and experience that God is in everything.

And very much important, I cannot create his presence

whatsoever. His presence in my life is always a gift from himself which I only can accept through faith. I have no grip on God and his closeness to me at all.

Furthermore, experiences of God, closeness to God, communication with God, to be in the presence of God, in the first place means interaction with the Bible text. We believe, and therefore it is only by faith, that God communicates with us through all the different stories and different literature we find in the Bible. We believe that God revealed himself through the ages in the history of people, and that history of God with his people was written down in the literature of the Bible and the history of the Church. To hear the voice of God, to discover him close to me, means therefore in the first place to listen very carefully to the stories, history, poems, etc., which we find in the Bible. And somehow – call it a mysterious way – God through his Spirit works some connection between my life story and the stories of the Bible.

It is important to make it very clear that the above mentioned interaction with the Bible, does not mean that even my best effort to listen to the stories of the Bible can itself create the so-called connection between God and me. Experiencing the presence of God is always a miraculous, mysterious creation of God!

According to my tradition therefore, all other so-called experiences of God are always under suspicion. I was taught to distrust all contemplative, meditative activity where the Bible is not the medium for our focus on God. On what basis should I put my faith in any form of meditative activities, because when, where and how are they sanctioned by God, revealed by him through Scripture?

I say this in reaction to some of the literature I had read on silent prayer. In this connection I stumbled on Anthony de Mello, somebody I respect very much. For example, from his point of view the well-known awareness exercises in themselves are forms of contemplation (body sensations and breathing sensations), which result in a so-called 'direct knowledge' or communication with God. As de Mello states it, 'In addition to the mind and heart with which we ordinarily communicate with God, we are all of us endowed with a mystical mind and heart, a faculty which makes it possible for us to know God directly . . . and furthermore, our indirect contact with God through images, concepts, is always a distorted reality of God' (Sadhana 25).

In my opinion every single way of experiencing God is in any case distorted. The point is, on what basis can I believe (and remember I am living by faith on the basis of the Bible) that, for example, the awareness of my body and breathing sensations are in itself direct experiences and communication with God that is not distorted? From my point of view de Mello is busy with pantheism.

What then does contemplation, or silent prayer, mean to me? Awareness of God.

Contemplation refers to a very simple experience. It is easy to understand. God gives this biblical contemplation to all who will accept the gift. He does not reserve it for a few specially chosen mystics or especially holy people. Contemplation is like the bread in the Eucharist in that it is given to all God's children.

To explain this contemplation let me refer to a familiar experience from everyday life. All of us have moments when we are struck into awareness by some natural phenomenon. Walking in a wooded valley you approach a stream. You are not particularly conscious of the stream until, coming to a place where the water rushes over the rocks, you are caught by the sound of water. For a moment it seizes your attention. It seems as if the babbling water is telling a very important message, but in a language you do not understand. You are drawn to listen closely, to attend exclusively to the lovely sound. In some way your heart does understand what the sounds of the water mean, even though your head cannot translate the message into human language. You simply say, 'It's beautiful.'

That first instant of awareness, before we begin to formulate thoughts and words, when we were simply and exclusively engaged in concentrated loving attention: that is the contemplation we are speaking of here. It can last a longer time, but ordinarily and typically it lasts only seconds or a few moments. Then we have our usual resource to thoughts and words about the beauty we have seen or heard. We quickly descend from contemplative gaze to reflective mental or verbal description of what we have seen.

In the same sense there will be times when the Word of God strikes us to awareness of the Divine Mystery. The contemplative awareness may last seconds or moments; rarely, if ever, it may last hours. What is it like; how can it be described? It has the character of being sudden and unexpected. It must not be striven for or greedily sought. It is a special visitation by the Word. He comes in this way when and as he chooses. Our part is simply to welcome him when he comes. We are not responsible for his coming. We are responsible to be awake, alert, ready to open immediately when he knocks.

The contemplative moment is an experience of illumined consciousness. It is a heightened awareness of God. It is a brief time when you are totally occupied in being lovingly aware of God. You are united with him now, but not by means of word and thoughts of Scripture. These thoughts and words have stirred you into an awareness of God himself. Suddenly you are overcome by the wonder of God Incarnate, walking, wearying, sitting on the ground by a well. It is awareness of him in a gift of concentrated attention. The person receiving this contemplation has no desire to read or think or speak. He or she desires only to celebrate his or her loving attention to God. This kind of knowledge is most deep and broad, having the mystery of God as its object. It is correspondingly poor in quantity and distinctness of thoughts. This contemplation knows God: it does not think thoughts about him. And so, after this experience all we can say is that we were lovingly aware of God, of his Love, of his Goodness, of his Son, of his Presence, of his Being, or some such global description.

Let us desire this contemplative gift humbly, realizing that no creature could merit or produce it by its own actions. It is not a reward we can win by our good works. It is always and purely God's gift. We become disposed for contemplation by giving ourselves to each instant of life in the fullest measure of the faith and love of which we are capable.

Who am I?

RACHEL NOEL

(Written during a 'creative session' at a JM retreat)

Do you know who you are?
Of course I do, what a silly question.
No, do you really know who you are?
If you look behind the labels society's hung round your head.

Wife, daughter, friend, eccentric, confused . . .
These are all just masks I wear, different roles I play, different tunes I sing.
But do they define me?
Do these labels dictate who I am?
Am I just an actor playing a part,
Saying words decided by someone else?
Does my whole self depend on a round of applause?
Does my being happy depend on someone telling me I'm good?
If they tell me I'm not, does that mean I'll be sad?
What if I see no-one, what will I be then?
How will I know to be happy or sad?
Am I just a puppet, suspended on strings,
Being pulled this way and that by passers by?
Do I have thoughts of my own? Any choices to make?
Does society determine who I am?
Surely there's more to being me, to being alive.
These labels will change as time goes on.
They define my relationships, my mood,
But all these will pass, they'll change.
They can't be who I am.
If I stop being a friend or being confused,
Does that mean I cease to exist?
It can't do.
But if it doesn't, then who am I?
Who am I, if I look behind the mask?
Who am I, if not defined by these labels?
Help me, Lord, to know who I am.
I need to know because I want to love.
To love I need to put others above me.
How can I do this, how can I die to self if I don't know who I am?
Oh Lord, help me to become aware of who I am,
Help me to be brave, to strip away the labels I've used to define me.
I'm scared, Lord, can we take this gently?
I've got a lot to learn, a long way to go.
Lord, take me step by step on this voyage of discovery, I want to love,

Not a shallow love, full of clichés I've learned,
I want to love how you would love.
Show me, Lord, teach me your love.

Positive and negative in meditation

ADRIAN B. SMITH

It would seem that set-backs, weaknesses, frictions were part of God's plan to enable the evolving process to happen.

When I began to learn physics at school, one of the first things I learnt was that unless there was friction between objects there could be no movement along a surface. If there was no friction between the soles of my shoes and the floor I would not be able to push myself forward. (We may have discovered the non-friction predicament when we first began to roller or ice skate!) Fire was created by our ancestors discovering the effect of friction when two pieces of wood were rubbed together.

In human relationships friction between people is regarded negatively. Yet here too it can be a cause of movement, of progress in relationships. Disagreement, disharmony, annoyance are bound to arise when two or more imperfect human beings with the limited understanding that our human condition imposes, try to be 'of the same mind'. But the outcome of such friction can be either negative or positive. It is positive when the occasion is used to grow in understanding, to broaden one's views, to draw closer together through dialogue. It is negative only when it is allowed to become the occasion of disharmony.

So friction is not, as our common use of the word suggests, always a bad thing. It is not in itself negative. If it has a good side, it must be part of God's creation: one of creation's ways of causing progress. St Paul suggests this when he speaks about the whole of creation evolving, through pain and groaning, to reach its glorious fulfilment.

For creation was condemned to lose its purpose, not of its own will, but because God willed it to be so. Yet there was the hope

> that creation itself would one day be set free from its slavery to decay and would share the glorious freedom of the children of God. For we know that up to the present time all of creation groans with pain, like the pain of childbirth. But it is not just creation alone which groans; we who have the Spirit as the first of God's gifts also groan within ourselves, as we wait for God to make us his children and set our whole being free. (Romans 8:20-3)

It would seem that set-backs, weaknesses, frictions were part of God's plan to enable the evolving process to happen.

Can we not apply this understanding to 'thoughts' during meditation? At first they seem only to be an annoyance, an impediment to our contemplation. We even label them 'distractions'. But we need to accept them positively. Their intrusion is the mind's way of purification: they are a means of unstressing, and consequently of growth. The deeper our mind goes while meditating, the more will our unconscious mental junk be caused to float to the surface. Maybe the thoughts that surface are full of anger (we imagine ourselves having arguments, writing angry letters) indicating that we have a deep, perhaps suppressed anger within us. Their surfacing during meditation is part of the process of our evolving. They tell us we have an emotion that we need to take note of. Be grateful! When such thoughts come to our awareness during our time of meditating, we do not get rattled: we just put them aside gently and resume our meditation.

None of us finds it easy to accept the painful fact that we are full of stress, any more than an oyster would approve of having grit under its shell. But for the friction caused by the grit there would be no pearl.

Not every meditation is a joy and a delight. While some meditations will seem to be light-filled (en-lightened), others, the majority perhaps, can be thirty minutes of boredom, of darkness. If it were not for the blackness of the night sky we would never be aware of the canopy of stars that are always above us.

Meditation at Heathrow

HAZEL POOLE

It calls up a vision of the great globe held in God's love.

The college where I make my annual retreat lies directly under the incoming flight-path to Heathrow Airport. Not the best centre for a retreat, you might think, as every few minutes an aeroplane roars overhead! Yet at a 'Pray through Clay' Retreat, this experience became for me a source of inspiration.

How come? Well, watching the aeroplanes reminded me that they are homing in from the North and South Poles, from China, India, the Middle East, Africa, the Americas – indeed from all points of the compass. For a short time they stay at Heathrow for unloading, reloading and refuelling and then soar up and outwards to every part of the earth. This is an amazing thought and calls up a vision of the great globe held in God's love. 'He's got the whole world in his hands.'

Aeroplanes and other forms of modern communication have brought us all together. So I took a lump of clay and made an orange-shaped globe held in the hands of God.

But other planes, in war, wreak appalling destruction and are instruments of human greed and hatred. With their nuclear warheads they even threaten to destroy the greater part of God's beautiful earth. So I took another lump of clay and broke it into small pieces, symbols of division and conflict: a shattered world.

Yet out of all this springs always the Christian hope of redemption and restoration. At our daily midday Mass, twenty or so of us homed in like the aeroplanes. We sat in a circle looking towards the bread and wine in the middle, symbols of the Body and the Blood. We passed the elements around to one another, united in the love of Christ. I modelled a loaf of bread and a chalice of wine. Then each one of us became a little aeroplane. Our noses pointed to the healing centre, our wings reached out to one another. Our tails faced the world outside the circle, wanting not to exclude others, but to share with them the gifts we are given.

Out in the open there were little 'planes': some representing people of other faiths, pointing inwards and wanting to share with us what they can teach us of Christ that we have missed. Others wandered rather aimlessly and some deliberately faced outwards, firmly rejecting the precious gifts.

So what began as a rather irritating intrusion into my retreat became and continues to be an enriching enlargement of my awareness of God's love for us all.

From stillness to silence

ANDREW LANE

> *If you are weak in a particular area then you learn the skills and you achieve good results. The problem is that this does not work with silence.*

The world of silence is one which has many mysteries and outwardly has many attractions, particularly for Christians leading a busy life in a busy world. The problem is that for many of us the way of silence is a hard way. One of the problems that has to be faced is that as I begin to enter something deeper, I congratulate myself on how I am doing and then crash, bang, I am back to square one. The truth which is so obvious and yet most of us take so long to learn is that, 'I cannot reach God by my strengths and abilities'. I need to have a humility of spirit which says that I cannot reach God. It always has to be the other way round. The first step, therefore, is to acknowledge my weakness. Then, and only then, God can reach out and touch me and enter into the core of my heart.

The second problem that faces me is that I am ill-equipped to face this world of silence. I have been brought up in the modern world with all its teaching and that does not help. Society judges success by very different methods and indeed so does the Church. 'Has your church paid its quota and more to the point, paid it in full?', 'Are communicant numbers rising?', 'Are church numbers going up?', 'Do you have prayer groups, Bible study groups, etc., etc., and do you attend them?', 'Do you use the latest communication skills and technology at your church?' . . . The questions are endless – but the inference is the same: are you good at it?

Strangely perhaps, as I travel around the Church, the answer to most of these questions is, 'Yes': the Church on the whole is good at it – and if they are not sound in all areas, delegation and enabling skills can cover the weaknesses. The point I am making about society and the Church is not a moral one but an educational one – if you are weak in a particular area then learn the knowledge and the skills, find yourself a good guide, director, counsellor or friend, and you will be able to achieve good if not excellent results. The problem is that this methodology does not work with silence.

Some might say that if you make God the guide then the above theory can work even for silence. I think that this is to miss the point. The 'I' (that is me) who wishes to learn from God, still remains the subject of the quest. Also, I believe this is to miss the point of what I discover in that great silence.

In the silence am I giving something to God? In the words of the carol:

> What can I give him, poor as I am?
> If I were a shepherd I would bring a lamb;
> If I were a wise man I would do my part;
> Yet what I can I give him, give my heart.

What does the last line mean? If my heart were of pure gold then fine, but anyone receiving my heart would need convincing that this is a gift of any value at all. If I am not giving a gift, is God giving me a gift? Again the answer is no, there is no gift from God.

In that deep silence when I meet the true and living God, the gift is not from God, the gift is God himself, in his entirety. When I am silent God does not speak to me, nor does he reveal himself in any way, and yet he gives himself. He is there, within me and as I allow that silence to well up it overcomes the noise, the rush, the bustle, and for a moment, I become one with God, I am God, for I am a child of God and I am one with the Son who went before me.

I am establishing a relationship, one in which I am dependent on the risen Christ. In all true prayer the presence of Jesus in the Spirit is at the heart of it. I leave you with two statements written by Carthusians which bring me comfort and yet fill me with trepidation as I attempt to allow God to remove me from silence to stillness:

Prayer is not an elegant stroll along the high places of the Spirit, but a return to the deepest source of our entire being; flesh, soul and spirit. This source is the Divinity which comes to us in the Spirit sent by the risen Son from the bosom of the Father.

Let us cast ourselves into the abyss and believe in the Absolute.

(*The Wound of Love*, DLT, 1994)

Unworthy though we are, let us continue into silence . . .

Wrestler

NICOLA SLEE

This, this is the place.
Seek love here, where
love is displaced,
overcome by fear. Dare

to look again. Face
again the stark wall
that blocks out all space.
Welcome dark. Fall

to fear that gives you chase.
Clasp your foe, hold
him in fierce embrace,
nor let him go. Fold

him to your chaste-
ned, beaten heart. Wrest
the blessing from his grace-
less lips. At once depart, lest

he should mark the face
turned to receive his gaze. Go,
hasten from the place.
The wound will always show.

The spiritual and the psychic

ROBERT LLEWELYN

It is unfortunate that many Christians are suspicious of the psychic . . . Psychic powers can be used selfishly for personal ends or benevolently for the glory of God.

What is the difference between the psychic and the spiritual? It is a question which, probably, most of us have often been asked. First we must understand how we intend the word 'spiritual'. The spiritual may be used in contrast to the physical, but I shall not be using it in that way. Used in that sense the question of moral worth would be irrelevant. The Archangel Gabriel and the devil (both being pure spirits) would be equally spiritual. I shall be using the word here in the New Testament sense.

Thus St Paul writes, 'to be spiritually minded is life and peace' (Romans 8:6). It is in that sense that I use the word 'spiritual'. There is no contrast here with the physical, for Paul is clearly speaking to those in physical bodies.

The spiritual person is the one who lives in the power of the Holy Spirit and who bears in his or her life the fruit of the Spirit: love, joy, peace, goodness, gentleness, forbearance, meekness, self-control.

The word 'psychic' has reference to paranormal phenomena: telepathy, psychometry, clairvoyance, tongues, healing, prophecy, etc. The psychic person may be deeply spiritual but this by no means follows. He may equally be a rogue, or perhaps controlled by demonic forces. It depends on whether psychic powers are used selfishly for personal ends or benevolently for the glory of God. Much psychic activity is morally neutral, the bending of spoons, for example: the psychic power works independently of whether the agent is a rascal or a saint. Two Gospel passages are worthy of attention. In Matthew 7:21-3 Jesus makes it clear that the capacity to work miracles is in itself no guarantee of goodness; and in Luke 10:17-20 he bids his disciples to rejoice not on account of remarkable powers but because their names are written in heaven.*

The devil is an example of a being of immense psychic power whose spiritual rating is zero. Jesus is an example of a person of the deepest spirituality possessing great psychic power. This power is made evident in such instances as seeing Nathaniel meditating under the fig tree, discerning the past life of the woman at the well, knowing from a distance that Lazarus had died, healing, exorcism, etc. But in him the psychic was totally subsumed in the spiritual. It was never used for personal ends but that God might be glorified.

Everyone is psychic to a certain degree, indeed every emotion, whether positive or negative, has a psychic charge. Communication in ordinary speech is in part a psychic phenomenon. But relatively few are psychic in the specialist meaning of the word as used here. Such are generally known as sensitives. Psychic powers may be developed but this is a dangerous thing to set out to do. However, it usually happens that as a person grows spiritually psychic powers do develop naturally without attention being paid to them, and this is safe and, further, beneficial because it is the spiritual by which the life is ruled. Even so, the degree of the psychic in a spiritually-minded person depends very largely on that person's psycho-physical make up and not necessarily on the depth of his or her spirituality. Thus in the realm of the psychic a rogue could be a giant and a saint a dwarf. Whereas, in the realm of the spiritual, gianthood would belong to the saint and dwarfdom to the rogue.

It must always be desirable that the spiritual should catch up with the psychic since it is upon the spiritual that salvation depends. Whether it is desirable for the psychic to catch up with the spiritual is best left to the Holy Spirit in the ruling of one's life.

The following from Dr Martin Israel makes a valuable summary: 'The gifts of the Holy Spirit are essentially psychic in nature (and in no way to be belittled on that account), but the harvest of the Holy Spirit is genuinely spiritual, by which I mean leading one to an encounter with God. Psychical gifts are excellent provided they are spiritually, and not egotistically, directed.'

It is unfortunate that many Christians are suspicious of the psychic. The word itself is morally neutral signifying neither good nor bad. It is the character of the one who uses psychic gifts, determining the end to which they are put, which makes them a force for good or evil.

* Note: The Revised English Bible renders the first passage: 'Not everyone who says to me, "Lord, Lord" will enter the kingdom of Heaven . . . When the day comes many will say to me, "Lord, Lord, did we not prophesy in your name, drive out demons in your name, and in your name perform many miracles?" Then I will tell them plainly, "I never knew you. Out of my sight, your deeds are evil"!' The second reads, 'The seventy two came back jubilant. "In your name, Lord," they said, "even the demons submit to us." He replied, "I saw Satan fall, like lightning, from heaven . . . Nevertheless, do not rejoice that the spirits submit to you, but that your names are enrolled in heaven".'

Being honest with God

ANGELA ASHWIN

> *God always comes to us at our point of need, not at the places where we are being worthy or respectable.*

Some time ago a friend told me that her small grandson had just been diagnosed as having a rare and probably fatal blood disease. In her shock and grief she was struggling to find some way of praying with so much pain. 'But I don't seem able to find God at all,' she said. 'I'm just so angry.' I suggested that she might dare to make her anger into an offering of prayer for Sam (not his real name), since this was the one thing she could give to God with all her heart at that moment. I also gave her a wooden 'holding cross' which she could literally hang on to when she could find no words. The act of holding the cross would itself be prayer.

She wrote later, describing how she had sat down and wept, telling God exactly what she thought of him. She had expected to feel ashamed for exploding to God like that, but she was surprised to find that her only sensation was one of numb exhaustion. Next day she felt that her praying had moved on, and she realised she was being asked to stay there, in the misery, with God. 'It was like allowing a stream of pain to flow through me,' she wrote. 'I didn't resist it, and I held on to that cross. It made all the difference that God had let me shout and scream at him yesterday, and hadn't rejected me. Now I'm beginning to glimpse a bit of God's love again, though it's hard work hanging on to this.' Her letter reminded me of some words of Melvyn Matthews (himself quoting Karl Rahner), '"Sometimes prayer is bleeding", and its source the incompleteness of the human person.'

When we come face to face with a crisis, either our own or someone else's, it is tempting to hide behind pious platitudes or explanations in order to try and make things all right and let God off the hook. But this won't do. A nurse told me recently that she witnessed a scene where a baby had just died and the priest said to the parents, 'It's the will of God.' The father punched the priest and knocked him over. Who can blame him? It is perhaps wiser to acknowledge that we are face to face with mystery in such circumstances, and simply to stay in the darkness with those who are going through hell. I am convinced that the prayers of my friend for her grandson Sam were powerful and real precisely because she had not pulled any punches with God, nor had she run away from the uncomfortable truth of the situation. Intercession is often a costly business, and it is right that this should be so. Our feelings of helplessness and frustration are themselves a vital part of our prayer because we are sharing something of the misery of those who are feeling lost and afraid.

So I believe that God's healing energy of love is more likely to be released into a situation when people have been given space freely to express their pain and anxiety. For those of us ministering to them, it feels like weakness when we do not produce pat answers to questions like 'Why is this happening to us?' But by refusing to run away, and by communicating God's love through our attitudes and actions, we will probably help them more than if we start theologising at the bedside.

There are of course moments when people do want to think through the implications of suffering and illness, perhaps some time after an acute crisis. Then it is appropriate to discuss the mystery of life on this planet, where bacteria are necessary but can wreak havoc, where living cells become cancers, where water can save life or drown us, and where volcanoes keep the earth sustainable.

I was greatly helped by the insight of a man who had suffered from arthritis for years. He said that he was quite sure that his illness was not the direct will of God, although God certainly wanted him to be alive. He saw it like this: just as parents allow their children to go out cycling, but do not directly will an accident to happen, so God puts us in a world where simply to be alive is a dangerous business. But God never deliberately causes us to suffer in it.

This is confirmed by the way Jesus' entire ministry was given to relieving human suffering. It is impossible to explain away pain and disease, but we can be clear that God never wills anyone to be sick or damaged because it might somehow be good for them.

But then we move back into total mystery, because there are cases where people grow and blossom through illness, and marvellous reconciliations take place in tragic situations between people who would otherwise never have come back together. This is itself healing, and we need to go on praying, holding in tension the darkness of human pain and an ultimate trust in the power of the divine love.

Some kinds of prayer, though well meant, can impose an intolerable pressure on sick people. Someone whom I shall call Susan had serious tumours on her spine. She has now made a full recovery, and was upheld and strengthened by the prayers of many over the long years of treatment. But there was a phase when she reached a very low ebb, at a time when members of a prayer group from her local church were visiting her. In his prayers, the leader kept asking God to increase her faith, so that she would 'claim the healing that was already hers'. She wrote to me, 'What if I don't get well? I'll feel it's my own fault, on top of everything else. They don't give me a chance to say how hellish it all is.'

If we can enable people facing illness and unhappiness to feel confident enough to express their vulnerability and fears, the channels are opened up for the Holy Spirit to work, far more than when we attempt teeth-gritting acts of 'faith' in our own strength. The very act of spitting out to God our dark and difficult emotions has a cleansing effect. There is a sense of release and relief because there is nothing left to hide. Sometimes old hurts and guilt will also come to the surface, so that there is now a chance to address these things, letting them become 'green', i.e., disposable, and leading to new growth, rather than a toxic irritant poisoning the system. And the wonderful thing is that God does not say, 'Tut, tut, you really shouldn't talk to me like that!' Instead we find ourselves scooped up into the enfolding of the presence of the divine love, as God says to us, 'Did you really think you could make me stop caring for you?'

By being completely open with God, we identify and expose to him the very things which most need to be touched and healed. God always comes to us at our point of need, not at the places where we are being worthy or respectable. We are in good company when we shake a fist at God. 'How long, O Lord?' rages the writer of Psalm 89. 'Will you hide yourself for ever?' The prophet Jeremiah even accuses God of being a 'deceitful brook' that has dried up on him (chapter 15:18). If these great friends of God can pray bluntly, so can we.

Obviously being angry with God is not a formula guaranteed to bring results, any more than any other way of praying would be that. We may be stunned and drained rather than angry, and feel more inclined to weep quietly than to wrestle with God. What we all need is the freedom to expose our deep and often conflicting emotions to God without fear. Then this becomes a step towards facing the situation and allowing God's healing power to flow into every aspect of it.

A parable

ERIC HAGUE

The Master of the garden took Bamboo and cut him down and hacked off his branches and stripped off his leaves and cleaved him in twain and cut out his heart. And lifting him gently, carried him to where there was a spring of fresh, sparkling water in the midst of the dry fields. Then putting one end of broken Bamboo in the spring and the other end into the water channel in his field, the Master laid down gently his beloved Bamboo. And the spring sang welcome and the clear sparkling waters raced joyously down the channel of Bamboo's torn body into the waiting fields. The rice was planted, and the days went by, and the shoots grew, and the harvest came. In that day was Bamboo, once so glorious in his stately beauty, yet more glorious in his brokenness and humility. For in his beauty was life abundant but in his brokenness he became a channel of abundant life to his Master's world.

Prayer at night: a thanksgiving

GAIL BALLINGER

The night's knife is sharp, whittling endurance,
Paring pain into prayer –
Prayer beyond pain; prayer beyond prayer almost,
Apprenticed to poverty
Pinioned in peace.

Captive, I live the night slowly,
Pray the night slowly, sleepless.
Wanting pours into waiting: a kind of awe
Stirred by winds of Spirit's searching,
Stilled by hidden flame.

The night is dark, alive in its own black brilliance,
  kingfisher clear,
And in the darkness my little love, world wounded,
  is grown into
A greatness not its own
Into a passion and purpose beyond my knowing,
Welded into oneness with Christ's constant interceding.
Heart of Spirit's pleading.
Seared by hidden flame.

That love reaches out
Beyond the known loves of family and friends,
Beyond the confines of cherished causes,
Beyond cost and comfort,
To enfold a world's weight in the holding of a name
In the power of hidden flame
Sharing the darkness.

Night streams softly into silence, the colour of praying,
Filled with Word of Father's saying,
Filled with wind and flame.

In acceptance lies peace

BROTHER RAMON SSF

I will forget those dying faces,
The empty places of those I have loved;
I will forget past days of joy,
Running along the hard sand at the sea's edge
And all the bliss of physical vitality and strength.
  But not in forgetting lies peace.

I will fill my life with action,
Crowd my days with occupation,
Involve myself in human endeavour and faction,
Filling each moment to justify my existence
So that others may think well of me.
  But not in endeavour lies peace.

Then I shall withdraw from the busy world
Stop worrying over people and events I cannot influence;
I shall shut my door and admit no love,
And crush all heights and depths of joy or pain,
Retreating, self-absorbed, from humanity.
  But not in aloofness lies peace.

At last, let me confess it – I am defeated;
There is nothing to do but resign and submit to my fate.
Health, joy and hope have been taken from me,
Empty and heavy with sadness, I give in,
For life's fire is all but extinguished.
  But not in submission lies peace.

Then suddenly, a ray of light pierces my gloom,
A spark of hope ignites strange joy in my heart:

I will accept my grief, pain and limitation,
My broken heart, yearning for love,
And all the breaking waves of sorrow;
For God will explain them all tomorrow
And lead me into inexpressible joy.
Here, in acceptance lies peace.

Brother Ramon died on 5 June 2000. He had been suffering from cancer. He sent us this poem shortly before he died.

Easter Reflections

EDDIE ASKEW

Peter in Gethsemane

The wound healed.
The sword washed clean.
No visible sign remains.
Only the violence within
and the unknown thoughts
of the high priest's servant.
When is healing complete?

Mary Magdalene

Did Mary ever garden?
Dig the cold earth,
sow seeds into damp darkness?
And wait?
Did she take cuttings
and slant them,
plant them like crosses?
Then watch for life budding from dead wood?
And in the garden
in the morning light,
when hope was dead and dry,
was the stone of grief
rolled away in sudden blossoming?

SECTION FIVE

'There are many beginnings': life stories

An unexpected pilgrimage

TONY HAWES

> *I had planned to go to the Holy Land . . . instead, I was to experience the Risen Christ.*

It is 5 a.m., Tuesday 11 May, 1993. The day we have been looking forward to for many years has finally arrived. Today we are off to the Holy Land. Our suitcases are full of lightweight clothes, high-factor sun cream, extra films, a bottle of kaolin, insect repellent, and flip-flops to walk over the rocks to the Dead Sea. We are, of course, wearing the obligatory sun hats.

The taxi arrives. We drive through the early morning to the pick-up point. A few members of the party are already there. Soon we are joined by the coach. We quickly get to Gatwick, and check in for our flight. Security is very heavy. We are X-rayed and frisked four times. We finally take our seats on the Monarch airbus. We observe our fellow travellers – Britons, Jews, Arabs and an assortment of other nationalities. Some are old, many are young. Some men have large black hats and long beards. Soon we fasten our seatbelts. We are on our way! Next stop Tel Aviv. Then Jerusalem, Bethlehem, Nazareth and the Sea of Galilee.

We chat to our neighbours, read, eat our lunch. Suddenly, with no warning, there are strange feelings in my head. Everything goes black.

The next thing I remember is being surrounded by several anxious people. I am having oxygen. I am moved to a three seater to lie down. Again I am overcome by that awful blackness: I learn later that I had no pulse.

Two good doctors on board recommend that I go to hospital immediately. An emergency landing is quickly arranged. The nearest airport is Bucharest in Romania. Romania? Yes. But I don't want to go to Bucharest, I want to go to Jerusalem! The aircraft seems to be making an almost vertical flight to the ground. I am suddenly terribly afraid.

We are met by a converted van, with a Red Cross painted on its side. Celia and I are bundled into the back, and suffer a fast bumpy ride to the hospital – the roads are full of potholes. I have visions of the back of the van opening and the stretcher sliding out onto the road.

At the hospital there are armed guards on the door. The interior is dark and uninviting. Not a word is spoken. I am wheeled into the small, ill-lit emergency room. The plaster is falling off the ceiling, the paint is peeling off the walls. A very ancient ECG machine is wheeled in and the electrodes are strapped to my body, Celia helping to hold them on. A very pleasant woman doctor takes the readings. She appears to be wearing a maroon dressing gown over her spotless white uniform. She speaks little English. I weep, not for myself but for her: how can she work under such terrible conditions?

The route to the Cardiac Unit is through dark corridors. Some of the walls are cracked from top to bottom. Through one of the few windows can be seen scaffolding holding up the main structure. The corridors are filled with people waiting. Visitors are not allowed on the wards. The State cares for your sick loved ones, and they are returned either healed or in a box.

The Cardiac Unit is small and sparse, but adequate. More terminals are strapped to my chest. I am connected up to a monitor and a drip is inserted into my arm. I lie there unable to move, dependent on those around me. I speak no Romanian and the staff have very limited English. Celia and I are to spend the next three days in a strange, poor, Communist-controlled, Third World land.

The material resources are few, but the love is great.

I had planned to go to the Holy Land to visit and explore the places where Jesus had walked, talked and healed nearly 2000 years ago. I had longed to stand in silence where he had been born, died and rose again for me, all those years in the past. Instead, I was to experience the Risen Christ, who walks, talks and heals among us today.

He was there in those concerned, anxious, loving faces on the aircraft. He was in that Cardiac Unit, with its minimum of equipment, as I was cared for by those dedicated doctors and nurses. He was there washing the floors, and emptying the bedpans. He offered me his shoes when I had none. He brought me food through those smiling kitchen workers – bread, rice, mint tea. I am certain he was with the doctor giving electric shock treatment to the young man opposite, bringing him back from death. He walked the ward at night, in that one night nurse – checking, touching, consoling. Language, politics or religious beliefs are no barrier where love is concerned. He was there too at the British Embassy, where staff comforted and cared for Celia in her distress. He was there with Worldwide Rescue as they brought us home. He was there as Celia held my hand, and in the faces of my two children as we finally stepped indoors. He came also in the many visitors, cards, letters and telephone calls, for which we are very grateful.

As I sit here outside in my garden recuperating, wearing again the obligatory sun hat, still not knowing what the future holds, again and again I keep hearing in my mind those words of St Teresa of Avila:

> Christ has no body now on earth but yours,
> No hands but yours,
> No feet but yours.
> Yours are the eyes through which must look out
> Christ's compassion on the world.
> Yours are the feet with which he is to go about doing good.
> Yours are the hands with which he is to bless now.

Amen to that!

'Trailing clouds of glory do we come'

JENNY MOULTON

> *When his needs are met the baby exercises a natural contemplative faculty . . .*

Becoming a grandparent is a bigger step on life's journey than I had realised, and has changed my perspectives on life. I had become focused on the complexities of mid-life, trying to make sense of past experience, and on the developing lives and careers of my two sons.

The arrival of the baby has given life a lightness and a wonder I never experienced in quite this way before. Perhaps because a grandparent does not bear the full responsibility for a baby, which can sometimes be overwhelming for the parents. The wonderful simplicity of life for an infant made more impact on me, being a stage removed from total involvement with the child.

Perhaps the greatest wonder was seeing how a baby can just 'be'. This is one of my deepest longings – to be truly myself as my Creator made me to be, and as I so often fail to be. It can be hard to keep in touch with the core of one's being, in the busyness of life – but this is a gift my infant grandson possesses from the outset, in his state of completeness and utter dependence. His dependence makes huge and insistent demands on his parents, but his needs are simple and basic. When they are met he exercises a natural contemplative faculty in his total acceptance of life as it is, and his knowledge that he is accepted as he is too.

Seeing my grandson, it is obvious that he is in touch with how he feels, and can express these feelings spontaneously, either negatively or positively! The division between his inner and outer worlds has scarcely begun. He has not yet learned to mask his feelings, a necessary and inevitable adaptation to life in this world. So often we learn to hide our feelings even from ourselves, and so deny their validity. By a wriggle of his body, or a smile lighting his whole face, my baby grandson conveys to me the pure wonder and joy of living – often a rare experience in the cares and trappings of adult life.

Part of a baby's appeal is its fresh, uncomplicated view of the world, which is unexplored territory in every sense. The appeal includes that inevitable spontaneity; unity of inner and outer life; contemplative disposition; joyful zest for life; simple trust; utter dependence. But the baby is an immature person. These wonderful gifts at the start of his life come to be left behind along the journey before, by the grace of God, they can be reclaimed afresh and with new depth when he has learned the hard lessons of experience.

Infancy is the beginning of the journey. The 'I am' of the baby is very different from the 'I am' of an adult. But I have come to see a correlation between the dependence and spontaneity of the loved and wanted infant, and the simple trust of the mature person who looks to God for his/her deepest needs and for the meaning of life.

Note: 'Trailing clouds of glory do we come' is a line from 'Intimations of Immortality' by William Wordsworth.

Unencumbered by luggage

YVONNE WALKER

> *Unencumbered, I learned to trust that the Lord will truly provide in abundance.*

Picture the scene – terraced sun-drenched gardens sloping down to the beach, swimming pool shimmering under the bright blue sky and a balcony with sea view. No, not a summer holiday, but a Quiet Day in St Brelades, Jersey. The hotel had opened specially for the occasion a week before the start of the Easter holiday season and forty people gathered for the Jersey Retreat Association Quiet Day, organised by Susan Halliwell who is contact person for two Julian Meetings in Jersey.

My theme for the Quiet Day was 'Our Waiting Journeys' and I suggested that we should start the day by looking at what we could leave behind, what is getting in the way, what do I not need, letting go the oughts, the musts, the busyness and just focus on waiting on God. An invitation to unload the excess baggage which we all carry around with us.

The irony of this exercise was that my actual luggage was sitting at Heathrow Airport, mislaid by British Airways. I had inadvertently been forced by circumstances to leave behind the notes, the hand-outs and the visual focus, all carefully prepared in advance, not to mention a change of clothes!

The Quiet Day was for me a very real lesson in letting go and travelling light. The time spent in careful preparation was not wasted as I hurriedly jotted down a few notes from memory the night before and as I went to sleep (in a borrowed night-dress) I handed the day over to God.

When we arrived at the hotel in St Brelades Bay, the swimming pool was just inviting a meditation on the healing at the pool of Bethsaida and the beautiful gardens were just crying out to be explored with a meditative walk enjoying the senses. An invitation, if ever there was, to unwind, let go and let God.

It was a great joy to share the fellowship, the deep silences, the quiet companionship of an unhurried, simple, delicious meal, the discreet, caring attentions of the hotel proprietor and staff, the sea breezes, the breathtaking beauty of the location and the shared experiences, often uttered as a single word, expressing how God had touched each one of us deeply.

For me it was an experience of learning to travel light in more ways than one: I had to let go of 'holding on' to my plans for a 'successful' Quiet Day, to my desire to control, to my carefully prepared framework. With no notes, no handouts, and no visual aids – unencumbered and going with the flow – I learned to trust that the Lord will truly provide in abundance.

My luggage finally caught up with me, three days late, in Guernsey, where I spent the beginning of Holy Week at Les Cotils, the retreat, conference and holiday centre in St Peter Port, situated in beautiful grounds just above the town. It was great to start each morning with a short time of meditation and worship shared with staff and residents in the 'upper room', a chapel with windows on three sides looking over to the other Channel Islands. I was also delighted to meet with and lead a contemplative prayer morning for members of the Guernsey Retreat Association who meet regularly as a contemplative prayer group.

The sacred in the ordinary

NANETTE BAILEY

Why was I so surprised to meet the Lord while doing the ironing?

On a lovely sunny afternoon I was ironing – not my favourite chore. I took some clothes to the airing cupboard and, as I re-entered the living room, I suddenly became aware of details I'd been oblivious to before: the sun streaming in, my three cats curled up asleep in an armchair. I also became aware of a feeling of very deep peace within the room. The feeling was so strong it felt almost tangible and within my heart leapt an answering flame of joy. I knew the Lord was here!

I savoured this atmosphere of peace and joy for a few minutes and as I continued ironing. I've often reflected on the unexpected gift of that golden afternoon. Why was I so surprised to meet the Lord in my home while doing the ironing? 'God is in all things' and 'the sacrament of the present moment' trip glibly off my tongue but I now realise I rarely live out those ideals. I rarely look for the mystery in the mundane, or the sacred in my day-to-day life, yet the Lord is as likely to come visiting while I'm washing the dishes or typing as he is while I'm in church or reading a spiritual book.

When the eighteenth-century hymn writer Ann Griffiths said what a pity it was that people would not 'come out of their ceiled houses to see the King of Glory passing by' she could have had me in mind. Every day the King of Glory comes to me but I am so often caught up in the 'ceiled house' of my own thoughts and busyness that I fail to notice him or appreciate the gifts he brings.

That golden afternoon taught me how much my spiritual eyes need to be washed clean so I can see into the depths of my ordinary life and see the treasures there. If I practise greater awareness I might, some day, appreciate in my heart that God is truly in all things: I may be able to reverence the sacrament of each moment.

Waiting at home

LYNN ROPER

I am so grateful that God has led me on this spiritual path.

I have always been drawn to quiet prayer, ever since my conversion, way back in 1975. Through the years, God has taken me on an interesting spiritual path, starting with the Church of England primary school I attended which faced the church and the graveyard. It was my special job to collect wild flowers from the church grounds for the nature table and in the peace and quiet of the morning sun, I happily gathered these beautiful creations, whilst the school assembly sang the hymn for the day. I like to think that perhaps God watched me and smiled, knowing that one day I would turn to him.

I attended church services after the baptism of my first son, being confirmed at the abbey at St Albans. I spent ten years in prayer and meditation at a Spiritualists' church in Luton.

Then I was led to All Saints' Church and happily joined the Julian

Group with my husband, and for six months I learned about this lovely movement and Mother Julian.

Sadly, due to health problems, I found I could no longer sit in chairs and I so desperately missed this time in God's loving presence that, against my husband's better judgement, I began the meditation nights at home. Just myself and my husband and a friend called Jenny who describes herself as not being a Christian but finding peace in the silence.

On occasions my two sons have joined in the group and they have both been helpful by showing respect for this special time in the home.

I really feel at one with this type of prayer, or meditation, and I am so grateful that God has led me on this spiritual path. It is hard to have a disability that prevents you from 'joining in' as I need to lie on a bed to meditate.

Last year I made a pilgrimage to Walsingham, visiting the Anglican and Roman Catholic shrines, and on my way home my husband took me to St Julian's church where I was able to thank God for so many things in the cell of Mother Julian.

The Julian Movement embraces so many different paths to God, and allows Christ to walk hand in hand with other faiths, bringing all souls united before God. It is a wonderful lesson in tolerance. If the world can unite in this way, then perhaps 'Peace on Earth' will one day arrive for all time.

How beautiful are the feet

JOHN HAWKINS

> *Reflexology has a powerful part to play within the healing experience of spiritual direction.*

In hot climates care of the feet is of crucial importance. For Jesus, there was both a healing and a spiritual significance in the washing of his disciples' feet, and the massaging of his own feet by a sinful woman.

Reflexology is an ancient therapy that was certainly known about in biblical times. It is based on the theory that the major organs and functions of the body are mirrored in reflex points on the feet. Massage and gentle pressure on these points can activate the body's natural healing energies.

After a profound healing experience four years ago, I decided to find out more about reflexology by taking a course, which has qualified me to practise professionally. My experience confirms that it 'works' – even if we don't know how (and that can be very irritating to those brought up in the western scientific tradition!).

It is also clear to me that as a wordless form of communication, reflexology has a powerful part to play within the healing experience of spiritual direction. That great mentor of prayer, Fr Christopher Bryant, used to say that the body was one's closest ally in prayer. Christians should not ignore what the so-called alternative therapies have to offer.

The 'phylum porifera'

JEAN DORRINGTON

> *There are approximately 5,000 described species of sponge and they inhabit all seas where they grow attached to hard rocky surfaces from the intertidal zones to a depth of 29,000 feet . . . Sponges have an extraordinary capacity to regenerate by restoration of damaged or lost parts.* (Encyclopedia Britannica)

The woman strolled along the edge of the gently receding sea enjoying her early morning walk. There had been a strong wind the day before and a stormy night, but now all was calm. Various pieces of litter were strewn on the damp sand and from time to time the woman stopped to examine something more closely. This time it was a sponge – larger than a tennis ball but easy to hold in her hand. She held it gently and reverently, fascinated by its intricacy, and wondered how long it had been tossed around in the sea before coming to land on this beach.

Lord, I know what it is like to be tossed about, detached from the rock that was my familiar place in life, tossed here and there by the storms of life, not knowing why the calm normality of life had suddenly changed. Why could I not have held on to the rock where I thought I belonged? Was my faith too weak to withstand the changing currents? Oh! to be back in those familiar surroundings and times. But eventually, things calmed down and I came to rest. The resting place was different, but it was a relief to be free of the storms. Then doubts crept in – for how long would I be calm and at peace in this unfamiliar environment? When would the storm start again? But I was gently lifted up, held lovingly and with reverence.

> Lord, keep me in your loving care and restore me.
> Open my ears to hear your guiding words.
> Remind me often that you made me and know me completely
> and that I am precious to my maker.
> Deepen my faith and trust, Lord, so that when the storms of life return
> I shall be rooted and grounded on the Rock of my Salvation
> and able to withstand the pressures.
> For it is in you and you alone
> that true peace is to be found.
> Lord, graciously hear and answer.

My glimpse of death

MARTIN ISRAEL

> *Coming back to myself, I knew that the supreme consciousness, which is one way of speaking of God, pervades all creation, and loves it . . .*

For five weeks in late June and July I was in a state of semi-consciousness caused by a severe neurological disease. The condition had developed insidiously over at least a year; the main symptoms were a progressive memory loss and an increasing difficulty in walking. I was already attended by a carer, but my rapid deterioration caused him intense concern. I became uncommunicative, incontinent, and I suffered total loss of memory. The amnesia was the worst part, as it cut me off from all contact with people. Instead I seemed to descend into a vast pit of darkness where I could 'sense' the souls of a vast concourse of people whom I did not know personally at all.

I seemed to be in hell, and I believe it could even be possible that this was literally true. There was despair, darkness, and a lack of communication between the souls that were there. The gloom was appalling, there seemed to be no hope anywhere. In fact I believe there was a total dissociation between my rational mind, which was shattered, and my spiritual mind which was forlorn and lonely but entirely free.

During this period many friends came to visit me, although I have no memory of this, and I received the Eucharist regularly from the reserved sacrament. On one occasion, I was anointed by a fine priest, Fr Bill Scott of St Mary's, Bourne Street, and this I believe marked the turning point of my survival, for I had lain in the balance between life and death for at least a week before.

The interesting thing about this entire period was a complete absence of fear, even though I was desolate and felt bereft of all human contact. Towards the end I am told that I became quite communicative at times especially with people I knew well, but I can remember nothing of this. I reached normal consciousness one morning in mid-July. It felt like waking up after a usual night's sleep, and I thought it was Monday morning. It was the ward nurse, who, somewhat laughingly, told me the true situation, that I had in fact been unconscious for five weeks. I was remarkably well orientated when I 'returned from the portals of death', but I was still suffering from partial amnesia and I had lost the ability to walk. I am still largely anchored to my wheelchair, but with the help of excellent physiotherapy and the constant support of my carer I have been able to walk with a frame, and even unaided.

Despite this terrifying experience, I thank God for the privilege of receiving it, because it has taught me so much and completely altered my personality and outlook on life.

I know that we are all immortal, not through our own deserts, but by the immeasurably great love of God. Of course, I have always known this on the mortal level. Being a natural mystic of great intensity I could not have thought otherwise, yet I could never entirely feel it in the depth of my soul. After I recovered normal consciousness, coming as it were back to myself once more, I knew that the supreme consciousness, which is one way of speaking of God, pervades all creation, and loves it, whatever its nature and use may be. For us humans there is an individual as well as a collective destiny and the end is glorious, but this incarnation is only one step towards that destiny which no one alive can know with authority.

Incarnate life, because the body is frail, is bound to be involved in suffering, and its intensity bears no relationship to the character of the person. But the way of suffering is an essential part of the progress of the person towards the self-knowledge and recognition of God – the second follows the first (Luke 17:21). No one knows what will happen to them when they die, nor can they in their present state, though it is permissible to speculate. But as it was revealed to Julian of Norwich, all will be well. The important matter in this life is that we live as perfectly in the present moment as we can.

All this is a basic aspect of the spiritual life of all religious traditions, without the punitive aspect so often stressed by fundamentalists. Heaven cannot be attained until we are all in corporate unity, and this requires a change of heart in every person. There will therefore, after death, be a fresh openness to divine reality. My entire attitude to life has been changed by my 'return from the portals of death', and I have ceased to be impatient with irritating people or disturbing circumstances. I have now acquired a degree of acceptance which makes every moment a joy in its own right.

Ichthus

ENID JONES-BLACKETT

Fish, great fish,
Jonah entered, passed through –
Fish,
multi-faceted, glided, curled, slid
in the ocean,
vulnerable,

swallowing
great gulps of water,

sifting the creatures.
Jonah asked
to be thrown, tossed away.
Jonah chose
to be one with the ocean.

Jonah, then, must pass through the fish.

Step into me, the fish-god,
outside scaled and horny,
succulent inside,
digesting the creatures.

I will spew you out,
I the fish-god.
You will be regurgitated, re-formed
but whole.

Like Jonah you can start again.

Then think again
of me, the fish-god,
swimming, sporting,
swallowing the ocean,
swallowing the creatures.
There are many beginnings.
Leap again.

SECTION SIX

'A pain by truth, a bliss by love': Julian and others

Julian's Cell

GLEN CAVALIERO

Dare one intrude? *Howsoever thou do*
thou shalt have woe: This arch survived
St Michael by the Thorn, a sure way
to stand upon that threshold
where were faced and reconciled for us
a pain by truth, a bliss by love.

Today the cell floor is too low
for one to glimpse an altar or a face.
She kneeled above where we peer in,
to endure that pain and understand
what glibly we can mouth: *all shall be well.*
Truth in a nutshell – as she saw

here, here in these few square yards
that framed for her the Lord of Kind
who would love and love more and burn
in the dialectic of desire. *If I might suffer more*
I would suffer more. In precious plenty
blood both signed and sealed that bond,

an issue of light on a pin-point
obliterating justice in a gust of joy:
sin is behovely. Flagstones ground her knees
where now good waxen polish scents
a marvellous mingling of weal and woe –
this faith, *which light is God our endless day.*

Light from a mystic

ROBERT LLEWELYN

For Julian, God's work is to love the hell out of us.

Julian of Norwich's spiritual classic *The Revelations of Divine Love* has been admirably summarised as 'a sublime and wonderful revelation of the unutterable love of God'. Yet Julian is not simply a devotional writer. She is also an astute and perceptive theologian. There is a distinctly modern ring, for example, to what she has written on the motherhood of God. Theology and devotion, as they always should, come together in Julian. Grace Jantzen said in her book *Julian of Norwich* (SPCK, 1987), 'Julian will settle neither for an undevotional theology nor for an untheological devotion.'

A cardinal point of Julian's teaching is the wrath-free nature of God. Those who think this makes Julian a sentimental writer with an insufficient regard to the seriousness of sin should reflect that she firmly insists on the reality of hell. But hell for Julian is not a place to which we may be sent by a wrathful God. It is a state in which we shall find ourselves if we do not allow God's all-compassionate love to quench the wrath within us. For Julian, God's work is to love the hell out of us. Hell is all that remains in us which is opposed to peace and love; wrath, as Julian terms it. If Julian were writing today she would doubtless say that we project our own wrath on to God.

Because God's love is pure compassion and there is no wrath in him, Julian is able to say that, theologically speaking, God cannot forgive us our sins. Just as I cannot come into my flat because I am already here, so God cannot forgive me my sins because he has already done so. It goes further than that. There was a time when I entered my flat, but there was no moment when God forgave me my sins. God's forgiveness has always been present, ready to be appropriated as I turn to him again. The change is not on God's part but on mine.

'When we pray,' says Julian, 'the soul is made willing and responsive to God. There is no kind of prayer which can make God more responsive to the soul, for God is always constant in love.' This truth that God forgives us before we repent, though we can only assimilate his forgiveness after we have turned again, is immensely liberating for those who can grasp it. It does not mean that we do not suffer, for we still need to be purged in the fire of God's love. What it means is that in our suffering God is on our side. And it is this which makes the difference between hope and despair.

Thomas Merton calls Julian a true theologian, meaning that her vision of God is true. Hers is the undistorted image. This is of vital importance to character and conduct because we become like the mental image we have of the object we worship.

If God's anger is to go, then his justice, as we normally understand that word, must be a casualty too. In a fallen world we need the concepts of justice and mercy to hold society together. No law court could function on the principle of the parable of the prodigal son, nor business flourish on that of the labourers in the vineyard. But God's ways are not our ways and in his dealings with us justice is swallowed up by mercy. 'True mercy,' Pope John Paul II has said, 'is the most profound form of justice.' As God's foolishness is more wise than human wisdom, so God's injustice is more just than human justice. And God's 'injustice' to us struggling people is his mercy.

To our proud natures maybe nothing is harder than to accept God's mercy. Instead, in mistaken humility, we tend to cling to our guilt and persist in self-blame. This is an unintentional dishonouring of God by denying the generosity of his love. Julian has strong words to say to us here. Our imagined humility, she says, is in reality a reprehensible blindness and weakness.

Julian has much to say on the motherhood of God. But she keeps the gender balance. 'As truly as God is our Father, so truly is God our Mother.' Julian never calls God 'she'. When we use personal pronouns of one another they are determined by the sexual characteristics of our material bodies. When we use personal pronouns in relation to God, who is pure spirit, they can refer only to traits of character. Our perception of God is enriched when we see that masculine and feminine traits find their integration in him.

We rightly stress the importance of the quality of prayer, but often forget the importance of quantity. Quantity belongs to us in a way quality does not. However hard I try, however much I want, I cannot recite a psalm with the love and devotion of St Antony. But I can, through grace, go on and on, thus 'psalming down the devil', as Antony puts it. All that Julian asks is that we pray with such devotion as is given us. No doubt from her own experience she speaks of perseverance (our contribution) in regard to prayer. She relates that Jesus told her,

> Pray inwardly, though you find no joy in it. For it does good, though you feel nothing, see nothing, yes even though you think you cannot pray. For when you are dry and empty, sick and weak, your prayers please me though there be little enough to please you. All believing prayer is precious to me.

Julian sees our human nature as basically good. When we practise deceit or lust we are being untrue to our human nature. We are perfectible not in spite of our human nature, but because of it. If I can be perfected because of my human nature, then spirit and body are partners in a common enterprise. Discipline remains necessary not because the senses are evil, but because they are so supremely good that God can never be satisfied with anything less than their full potential.

I have referred to Julian as a teacher but she would make no such claim. She wants to sink into the background. 'You shall soon forget me,' she says, 'and behold Jesus who is teacher of all.'

Sunlight and darkness

SISTER MARGARET MAGDALEN CSMV

The image that came to me was of sunbathing in God's love . . .

Some of you may have seen *Songs of Praise* when it was televised from Wymondham Abbey and perhaps felt, as I did, that the highlight of it was the interview with Father Robert Llewelyn, who for many years was chaplain of Julian's shrine at Norwich. Now in his eighties, he is still incredibly sprightly. Talking to Pam Rhodes as much with his large and most expressive hands as with his beautiful voice, Fr Llewelyn spoke of how God in his compassion loves the hell out of us, quite literally – his love burns up all the wrath, the selfishness, the proclivity to darkness and its evils. Looking at the sun streaming through the window he said, 'I can draw the curtains and shut out the sun, but I can never turn the sun into darkness. Similarly,' (and with that he folded his arms across his breast and bowed his head as though hugging himself in sorrow), 'I can try to shut out the compassionate love of God, but I can never turn it into wrath. It will still go on loving me until I pull back the curtain and allow it to penetrate and burn up the hell in me.'

The image that came to me was twofold. Firstly it spoke of sunbathing in God's love and being gently warmed right through by it. Secondly it spoke of being exposed to a kind of spiritual radiotherapy, or divine laser beam, that burned out the hell in me.

All of us must have experienced moments – special memorable moments, perhaps in a retreat – when we have felt as though we were exposed to a kind of radiation of God's love. Maybe we've basked in the wonder of it and gone around in a glow of joy for days! But as with radiotherapy, such experiences tend to be short and intense. We couldn't actually cope with that level of intensity for very long.

These moments are often followed by long and very dry periods of prayer – to the point where one begins to wonder if the overwhelming experience of being loved by God was spurious or artificially induced. We assent in our heads to the truth that 'the steadfast love of the Lord never ceases, his mercies never come to an end . . .' but it's hard to get excited about that, as a living part of one's faith, when the heart feels completely numb.

Julian herself reached her profound insights into God's compassionate love through a series of visions, and vision as we know is ' . . . an extortionate trafficker. Not content with demanding a price in advance, she exacts almost as heavy a price at the end. A moment of insight has to be paid for with months – years maybe – of spiritual aridity' (H. Herman, *The Meaning and Value of Mysticism*, James Clarke, 1915). John Bunyan also discovered that the blessings of God are often preceded or followed by darkness.

> Though God doth visit my soul with never so blessed a discovery of himself, yet I have found again, that such hours have attended me afterwards that I have been in my spirit so filled with darkness, that I could not so much as conceive what that God and comfort was, with which I have been refreshed.' (From *Grace Abounding to the Chief of Sinners*)

The fact that we do not feel God's compassionate love streaming to us through the window, as it were, is neither here nor there. It is nevertheless a reality. The mystics were all very familiar with darkness and aridity and faith-without-feeling. We too need to hang on in trust believing that God is not capricious in his loving.

All of that you probably know very well from long experience on the Christian journey. But I was grateful for the reminder through Robert Llewelyn that God was 'loving the hell out of me', even when I couldn't feel the 'sun's rays' or the 'divine radiation'. For he who himself 'descended into hell' and became fully acquainted with its horrors, knows just what to target in each of us.

In silence I found her: Julian the Solitary

MARY BLAKE

> A dark cloak about her
> an oak tree of a woman
> the fast river beside her
> her voice is the greenwood
> her staff a green willow
> her cell empty of clutter
> lay woman unlettered
> many have sought her
> few turn from her door
> the larks they are singing
> the bells they are pealing
> all shall be well
> and all manner of thing
> shall be well.

Circle dancing

ENA TAYLOR

> *Nourishing something within which one knows to be sacred.*

I have been a Sacred Circle dancer for ten years. We have a very enthusiastic group meeting weekly. My introduction to Julian of Norwich came through dance: *The Bells of Norwich*. Later, on visits to Norfolk, where I was born and lived for many years, I was able to visit Julian's cell twice. I also joined a group of handicapped circle dancers in Norwich. The joy on the faces of dancers who, as in the case of cerebral palsy sufferers, could only use hands, was quite humbling.

For the past three years, we have celebrated Julian in worshipful dance with her words, on the Friday evening closest to the eighth of May. This year the date chosen coincided with the celebration in Norwich, and also with the Festival of St Julian of Norwich held in the place of meeting at the church of St Julian of Norwich at Ballajura in Western Australia. As yet there is no church building – just a block of sandy soil. But in a nearby hall, temporarily used, we joined the congregation in an address, dinner, and finally, two dances: *The Bells of Norwich* and *Ein Lied vom Tielen,* known to us as the chalice dance.

People speak of the dance as nourishing something within which one knows to be sacred. The mystical dimension that transcends boundaries is more than apparent in the variety of dances both ancient and modern in origin, and of different sacred grounds.

Inner vision

HEBE WELBOURN

> *Contemplation involves all kinds of vision, external as well as internal.*

I sometimes find a kind of pre-verbal message welling up in me – we all do at times. We have the urge to write a poem or make a picture. When I make a picture I don't see it as on a television screen, it seems to come out of my hands from an inner pre-verbal idea. This is a common experience with people on creative retreats using paint, clay, collage, etc.

Another powerful kind of pre-verbal imagery comes to us in visualised meditation – as in an Ignatian-style imagination of a biblical passage, or the kind of guided visualisations used, for example, in Anthony de Mello's books. Most people use something of the same kind of imagination when reading a novel or listening to a radio play. We are in an imaginary world, surrounded by the scenery with its sights, sounds, smells, and feelings. We participate in the action, talk to the characters, are moved and changed by what we seem to see.

Dreams have a similar quality. We are in another quite different world. Sometimes we even seem to be a different person. The scene shifts unpredictably and none of the usual rules seem to apply. Sometimes they are just like a random debriefing of the brain, short-circuiting while resting from conscious control. Most of our dreams are forgotten and yet in some strange way they are important to us. If we take the trouble to remember and record them we often find they contain powerful messages.

To cultivate inner vision is to cultivate 'fool's vision'. We learn to look at things as if for the first time without putting any clever stuff between us and what we see. We use this kind of vision to some extent when driving a car or dancing with a partner or painting with the right side of the brain: paying very careful attention to what we are doing but without figuring it out from an instruction manual or consciously striving for technical brilliance. Fool's vision involves relying on the dark, unconscious, shadow side of us. Most of us are educated to be conscious, calculating and verbal. We find it hard to draw on our inner vision and feelings. We like to come to conclusions, formulate creeds and doctrines. The pain and the promise of incompleteness are often more than we can bear.

Contemplation ('beholding', as Mother Julian expresses it) involves all kinds of vision, external as well as internal. In the course of my daily life and prayer I engage in looking at things, making pictures, having prophetic visions, having useless visions, visual meditation, dreams, driving a car, dancing. My daily interactions and prayer have something of all these qualities. But, at the end of the line, all these images are let go and I am left with . . . nothing. In the dark. I used to worry that sitting in the presence of God, I was aware of no one there. Surely, I should put some beautiful object or beautiful thought in the centre, from which to start? No. Whether I bring with me pain, puzzlement or joy, I must let these go and just wait, in the dark. And without knowing how, I am seen, heard, held and energised.

Annie Dillard, in her book *Pilgrim at Tinker Creek* (Picador Pan, 1976), has some wonderful reflections and descriptions of our relationship with the natural world. I draw particularly on her chapters entitled 'Seeing' and 'Stalking'. Her description of stalking muskrats: 'I center down wherever I am; I find balance and repose. I retreat – not inside myself but outside myself, so that I am a tissue of senses . . .' The nearest I get to this is bird watching. Watching that bush, for what? I don't know. Might be anything. I'm so intent I don't know I'm here. The bird doesn't know I'm here. But be sure, if recognition comes between us, it will take wing and fly away.

Objective vision depends on having good eyes. Sometimes I take off my glasses so as to get blurry vision: pure masses of light, shade and colour not necessarily representing any image. Once I was given a pair of varifocal glasses with the wrong astigmatic correction and found my handwriting became sloped and elongated. They say that the heavenward thrust of El Greco's painting is due to astigmatism but I guess he was painting from inner vision. With my glasses on, I like to *really* look. Looking at a flower with watercolours at hand. The painting doesn't matter. What does matter is that I give the flower my undivided attention. I will notice the shape of each petal, the ruffling of its stamens, little movements as the bloom opens to the light, the recurring pattern of leaves and stem. Eventually the flower and I just look at each other, resting.

Then there's looking at pictures. I know of one person who uses pictures as a means of stilling her mind into prayer. She looks at the picture attentively, observing one part of it after another without comment until her attention is resting softly on the whole. Sister Wendy Becket, in her television series and in her book, *The Inner Gaze of Love* (Marshall Pickering, 1993), has much to teach us about the use of pictures in prayer.

Recently I have had occasion to make some study of Hildegard of Bingen. I also have visions. I guess a lot of people do, but we don't often talk about it. People say that, because some of her pictures are zig-zaggy, Hildegard's illuminations originated in migraine. I get migraine, but I wouldn't want to paint it. At best, the sparkling zigs are a nuisance because they come between me and what I am looking at. I also get hallucinations while meditating, especially if I am a bit drowsy. Sometimes Hieronymus Bosch is nothing to the little demons, funny people and voices I get beset by. They are a nuisance. They go away if I open my eyes, start again, calling upon my Centre with the Jesus Prayer. Sometimes I find myself looking into the centre of a vortex of spiralling beautiful colours. They may draw me into sleep, or I may just sit and watch them go by. Some people see pictures or writing very clearly, as on a screen. I think Hildegard's visions were of this kind. She described her visions to some monks who painted them for her.

The visions of Hildegard of Bingen were not just random sparklings of her brain. They were powerfully symbolic, archetypal, prophetic. Prophetic: like Isaiah and Ezekiel. She felt called as a prophet and is still venerated as such by those who study her visions.

The teachings of St Benedict

DON STEPHEN

> *The preparing of the meal was as sacred as the preparation of the Eucharist.*

St Benedict lived in about 540 AD in Nursia, Italy, and is famous for a rule that he drew up for monks or nuns living in community. Not only did this rule become the foundation of the Benedictine Monastic Order but it also shaped the very nature of the secular Church. The illuminated books and manuscripts all have their roots in Benedict, even the way the parish church or cathedral is built is Benedictine in concept.

He emphasised the custom of 'Hospitality'. Greet all who knock at the door as you would greet Christ, he says, and welcome them. But don't allow them to disrupt the household. And if they stay, put them on the duty roster, so that they too may work to support the household. And beware of those who go from house to house, place to place, living off the good services of others. Apt words for our age with its culture of hand-outs and of demands for rights and privileges without the equally important balance of hard work. For Benedict you greeted all who came to your door as if they were Christ, but you were very wary of those who would take advantage – for Christ would never do that, and his presence would bring blessing. So even the wayfarer was invited to be like Christ, bless the monastery or the house with his/her presence and labour.

He also wrote that the vessels of the kitchen are as sacred as the vessels on the altar – that all work, whatever it might be, if done in love, was a sacrament. The preparing of the meal was as sacred as the preparation of the Eucharist. In other words he invited people to find God in all things – the mundane, the everyday, as much as in the Pontifical High Mass.

The Benedictine tradition also developed a way of looking at the Bible which is still with us today. *Lectio divina* (divine reading) is what they called it. Simply, what it taught us is this. That when we read the Scripture or it is read to us, God comes and speaks his individual message of love to each of us. How it works today is like this:

As you read a favourite passage of the Bible, a psalm or maybe a section from the Gospels, wait for a word or a verse to stand out for you.

Then discard the rest of the passage and go back to that verse or word.

Read it again, mull over it, just play around with it in your mind.

Finally, sit quietly and ask, 'Lord, what are you trying to say to me here in these pages, here in this verse or word?'

Then sit silent, hear what he whispers to you!

The joy and strength of union: Thomas Traherne and God's holy days

A SISTER OF THE COMMUNITY OF THE HOLY CROSS, REMPSTONE

> *Some seasons and days are especially pregnant with God's presence . . .*

Holidays are not what they were. Now they are merely things that we go on, two or three times a year if we can, one of the ever-increasing number of rights we demand. Hard luck on those who don't get any at all but as long as we are all right and have something to brag about we don't get over concerned.

Not that there is anything wrong in relaxing and having a necessary break, meeting new people and seeing new things, enjoying the beauties of God's world. Burn-out is not a Christian virtue. Rather, what is largely missing in contemporary life is a sense of the sacredness of time, the realisation that some seasons and days, as well as some places, are especially pregnant with God's presence and activity and that for the sake of our spiritual well-being we need to savour them. God's healing power and saving work have to be appropriated by us, re-experienced as present reality in purposed rituals of remembrance. This is what an incarnational and sacramental religion is all about.

Mostly we are quite good on birthdays and on the anniversaries of the death of those we knew and still love. Jubilee celebrations of world events have also caught on. But so often it is God himself who is left out, as with so many of the Millennium celebrations. Whitsunday has been swallowed up by the Spring Bank Holiday . . . So it goes on.

Our forbears lived quite differently. Holidays were what they say they are, holy days, breaks from the round of work and routine to celebrate the things of God. Admittedly they got out of hand sometimes, but the intention was there. They were corporate occasions too, times for being together. It wasn't all that easy to feel left out in the more close-knit societies of former times.

All the same the real purpose behind the celebrations needed to be stressed. It is interesting to look, for example, at some of the things Thomas Traherne had to say in his seventeenth-century work *The Church's Year Book*. Writing as a Church of England priest and a man of prayer at a time when different emphases in theology and ecclesiastical understanding were competing for ascendancy, his obvious concern is to ensure that the value of liturgical celebrations, the keeping of feasts and holy days, should be recognised and therefore maintained. Why, he asks:

> . . . should we not spend some time upon holy days in contemplating the beauty of holy days in themselves?

And why shouldn't we join him and let the lyrical beauty of his writings inspire us to find again some of the treasures we have lost in our materialistic and sceptical age? We have got to start though from where we are. Holy days, like holidays, are given us to relieve monotony and add colour to our lives, if we are properly attuned that is. Traherne describes them as 'a grateful relaxation from cares and labours'. This won't be immediately obvious in our secular society which relentlessly sweeps everything along with it in frenzied activity. But as Christians we must resist all this and find ways and means of entering into our heritage. Such days, in truth, are:

> . . . the ornaments of time and the beauty of the world; The lucid intervals and lights of the year . . . seasons of melody, joy and thanksgiving.

If this seems a far cry from reality maybe we need to look into things and see why we are missing out. How real is our faith? Paradise certainly seems to have been lost, while Traherne sees the yearly round of feasts and festivals as 'relics of Eden and superadded treasures' but at the same time pointing forward as well to what is still to be:

> . . . days of heaven seen upon earth . . .
> The very cream and crown and repose of our lives
> Wherein we antedate the resurrection of the dead.

These days then are too precious to be frittered away. As far as we can we should seek to escape from the normal run of things:

> . . . come from our shops to our Saviour's throne,
> From ploughing our fields to manna in the wilderness
> From dressing our vineyards to the wine of angels
> From caring for our children, to be the sons of God.

Not that we are to drop everything in selfish indulgence, but maybe we could find just a little space to celebrate and let the mysteries of our faith seep into us. Our earthly preoccupations can be transmuted into another sphere. God comes to mingle among us at these times, these:

> . . . Market days of heaven.
> Appointed seasons wherein God keeps open house,
> . . . spiritual regions wherein we walk in the paths of God.

Possibly we can only find a brief interval to slip off on our own to pray. So be it. But if possible we could join with others in celebration:

> A private person is but half himself and is naturally magnified in others

For these holy days are:

> ... blessed opportunities wherein we come from our
> solitary closets to see ourselves in solemn assemblies,
> Single devotions are weak in comparison of these;
> here is the JOY and STRENGTH of UNION ...
> The difference between earth and heaven is that here
> we are dispersed, there we shall ever be united together.

Fellowship and community are so desperately needed in our fragmented world and it is precisely these things that we inherit as Christians. Holy days and liturgical celebrations enable us to experience in time what will eventually be ours in fullness. They are:

> Golden links uniting our souls and all things together:
> Apostles, prophets, patriarchs appear in them and come unto us.
> Moses, King David, and Solomon welcome us,
> Saints and martyrs visit us.

We taste already, if you will, the *joy* and *strength* of *union.* Yet we cannot take it all simply as a given. Merely to be there with one another doesn't always make for harmony and bliss! Our celebrations must not be mere jamborees to disguise all the underlying tensions. There must be silences, spaces for prayer and meditation, for penitence and for letting the Holy Spirit impart the mysteries of our faith to us in secret. 'Without contemplation we lose the benefits of the ages,' Traherne says. But he concludes by saying that without celebration together we also lose the benefits of contemplation. Holy days open up God's exchequer to us and:

> Without sanctifying these we lose the benefit and the end of our lives, which is to enter into the treasuries of God almighty, and to feel his love, and to offer up ourselves in joy and thanksgivings.

So it is that with Traherne we pray to our:

> Most Holy God, and author of all sanctity and lover of all unity, whose wisdom hath established an admirable communion between the Church triumphant in heaven and militant on earth ...

To strengthen us to resist the pull of earthly attractions and instead draw our strength from the truly holy days given us from him as *'earnests of our eternal rest',* where we shall *'all meet before [his] glorious throne to adore with one heart the Saviour of us all'.*

SECTION SEVEN

'A well to draw on at need': The Julian Meetings

A Prayer

Cuffley (Hertfordshire) Julian Meeting

Lord, we met here together
to try to find you.
We gratefully acknowledge
that you have found us;
as indeed you promised.

May we know your presence
with us in our homes
and in our gardens;
in the shops
and in our workplace;
as much in the city roar as in the mountain's peace.
Amen.

A new experience of prayer

ANN ECHLIN

The explanation of what we were about gave me confidence to discover what it is like to be open to God.

I had heard about Julian Meetings and knew that they were prayer meetings, but other than that I had no idea what happened. An invitation to go to a Julian Meeting sounded attractive. I have never found prayer easy. I have never been sure when I pray that I am doing the right thing. The opportunity to learn more about prayer and perhaps another way of praying led me to accept the invitation.

I went along not knowing what to expect or what demands would be put upon me. The informality, as we chatted over a cup of tea, helped. I knew some faces but on the whole this was a new group of people. The explanation of why we were there and what we hoped to do during the time gave some structure to the meeting and made me feel more comfortable. The teaching about contemplative prayer and the practical advice about how to go about it, how to relax, how to sit, to be alert yet not involved in thoughts and distractions reminded me of bits I had read and had picked up from other talks on prayer. The questions and comments from members of the group reassured me. The same questions went through my mind. How would I know if I was doing the right thing? What happens if thoughts rush in and my concentration goes? Was God asking me just to sit and wait?

The silence was not difficult. Numerous visits to Taizé have taught me the value of silence. Perhaps now I understand just what was happening in those long periods of silence. My problem was that I had tried to talk too much and not just let myself be open to God for long enough. The help of the 'anchor' word became so apparent as the thoughts and the desire to take over pushed in. At the end of the silence, as we were brought out of the prayer, I felt reluctant to move. I wanted to hold onto the stillness in me, the desire to be with God. That desire, I learned, was in itself prayer. Books and leaflets are useful, but the clear and quiet explanation of what we were about gave me confidence to discover what it is like to be open to God. I am glad that I accepted the invitation.

Journey to Julian

JOAN WILTON

> *There was a treasure hidden in a field somewhere, and until I found it there was to be no rest.*

It was the evening before Michael Ramsey was enthroned as Archbishop of Canterbury, and he was being interviewed at the end of the television news. 'And what will your prayers be?' he was asked. The eyebrows fluttered a little. 'Looking to God, looking to God all night,' was the reply.

The voice persisted, 'I expect you will be seeking guidance in this great task.' The eyebrows grew more agitated. 'Just looking to God,' he repeated. I switched off and sat still for a moment. What did he mean? It was something of immense importance to him of which I knew nothing. For most of my life, prayer was only asking God for help when the going got tough.

A few years passed, and I was on a parish retreat. On the last afternoon the conductor asked us, 'Is there anything you would like to discuss?' 'Some help with prayer,' was the immediate answer. He suggested that the Sisters of the Community would do it far better than he could, and so two came to see us. Their rule was to spend one hour in silent prayer together each day after their first office.

'But what do you do all that time? What do you say? How can you control all your thoughts? Don't you get stiff?'

They replied, 'We call it "Being here for God", and we just sit like contented beggars, expecting nothing, waiting.' Further questioning only produced the same answer, and they rose, smiling, and left.

We decided to try to do this ourselves, to spend fifteen minutes in stillness each day, and meet in a month's time. Only a few turned up then, and no one had managed more than six turbulent minutes. We tried once more: it was beyond our capabilities.

But a small flame had been lit. There was a treasure hidden in a field somewhere, and until I found it there was to be no rest. Where could 'Looking to God' and 'Being here for God' be found? In meditation perhaps. During the following years I tried anything that came my way: the local Christian Study Centre had a course on prayer; the Unitarians had meetings. They did not have the answer. Then someone came to see me from a group that met every Friday evening for an hour's silence. Was this it? She explained fully. 'I'm sorry,' I said. 'It's a very near miss. Thank you, but I must go on looking.' She left me two names and addresses. The first was 'Julian Meetings'. I wrote at once, asking for information and help. After three weeks there was no reply. (I learnt later that the letter had not been forwarded to a new address.) Five weeks passed; two months.

Meantime I discovered that Julian was a woman, a mediaeval mystic who had visions and said, 'All manner of thing shall be well'. In desperation I wrote to 'The Julian Cell, Norwich'. Immediately there was an encouraging reply from Robert Llewelyn, giving me the address of the nearest group; it was five minutes' walk away. I was nearly there. I rang in excitement and trepidation and went to the next meeting.

The experience of that first occasion has not faded. I was gently, firmly enfolded in a dark, deep embrace of silence. Time and breathing appeared to stand still; we were bound in a loving circle of unimaginable strength. The candle in the middle mirrored the tiny flame of years before. Here was the pearl of great price at last.

Our small group meets in each other's homes every fortnight; we worship in different churches. Enquirers sometimes ring and then lose their nerve; or come for a few times but find it is not for them; or come and stay. Older members move away, but in all its long life no one has ever been left alone. It is difficult to explain why these shared silences have such potency. But without them I know there would not be the strength to enter each day in the power of the Spirit, and armed against the rulers of the darkness of this world. We can only say, 'Come and see'.

A journey to silence

DEIDRE MORRIS

> *Increasingly, as silence and meditation have become an integral part of my life, God is also part and parcel of everything.*

If I go back to the early 1980s, I was a full-time wife and mother of two primary school children. I was a regular attender at church, took my turn on the coffee rota, and was busy in many church activities.

Then in summer 1982 or 1983 our church cleaner's family was in crisis. Along with others I helped keep things clean and tidy. One day our Deaconess phoned to say that the cleaner had decided she would not be able to come back – had I any ideas for someone to replace her? I thought and I prayed and phoned her to say that I would do the job. She protested – it wasn't my sort of job, she knew I didn't like housework much and it paid very little. Also I was a graduate, I could do so much more. I still said I wanted to do it, and she agreed to let me.

Why was I so insistent? I didn't know then, but I know now.

From then on I spent six hours a week in our church, with my hands busy and my mind and spirit free. Some weeks it was like working at Crewe station, there were so many people coming and going. But mostly I had six hours on my own, undisturbed. No one dictated what I did, or when, or how. So long as the necessary work was done I was free to organise it as I chose.

During the two or three years I did the job I came to love the silence and solitude; to value doing something unnoticed (in the main) to the glory of God; to have a focus for thought and prayer, as I worked surrounded by an amazing number of wooden angels and a myriad of Christian symbols. Of course I thought of lots of other things as well. But the atmosphere of a place long used for prayer and worship certainly sank deep into me. Being there at Sunday worship was something totally different.

When we moved to another part of the country, I missed this, very much. But life got very busy. And then I found that members of our new church went off on a silent retreat each year. Brian agreed that I should go first. The retreat was a revelation. Here really was silence and 'concentrated God'.

Then someone at church who already went to a Julian Meeting suggested we have a JM each Sunday in Lent. Brian and I went along. We continued to meet beyond Lent each fortnight. That was probably 1988. From then on, if we were at home we attended the JM, and ran it for a while when the initiators had other calls on their time. I think its attractions were:

(1) The silence. So little of our worship has this. So little in most people's lives has it. Most of us learn of prayer as petition, and talking to or at God, and many never get beyond this. Some people seem terrified of being silent before God and talk to or about God just to avoid the silence. JM taught me more and more how to use the silence that I had learned to value as I cleaned.
(2) The stillness. We are so rarely still but alert. It was by learning to be still and silent that I learnt to focus on (listening to) God, as opposed to talking at him.
(3) Being small and focused. Small enough to be close and get to know each other. A group not to do – like a committee, or the choir – but to be, together. Not judged by results!
(4) The freedom from structure, denomination, status and gender. We are all equal – giving and accepting within the group whatever the meeting's opener and closer would bring. There was

> no hierarchy, no rules, no special clothes, no ritual actions or responses. We were, essentially, outside the regulations of denominations.

In 1992 I moved to a different church, which also had a Julian Meeting, one which met monthly. So I joined that for the same reasons as above. Since we moved to Wales a year ago I have not been able to get a group started locally, but will persevere and hope, in God's time, that it will happen.

If JM had set a rigorous rule of meditation and life, I would certainly not qualify, and would probably never have started. I have since spoken to people who meditate for thirty minutes twice a day – I think they follow John Main's teaching, from what I could gather – and who were surprised that I did not. But I have never found it possible to fit it into the sort of life I lead. Does this suggest that I am not motivated to do so? Maybe. But it is how I am.

I do feel it is one of the strengths of JM that it is not prescriptive. That people are welcome to explore what is right for them, and right for them at this point in their lives. We are all different, and we change as we grow, so that life continues to be an exploration of how to approach God now, at this time. I find it difficult to accept that there is a single way that is right for everyone all the time. I think this approach helps some of those who are unsure of what they are seeking, and would be put off by too strict an approach, or demands to conform. Some people need the demands and discipline of a 'Rule', others are put off by it.

How has JM affected my personal spiritual life?

I have found belonging to JM has affected my daily life in that, before (I now realise, looking back), God was in a compartment labelled 'Sundays, church and prayer time'. Increasingly, as silence and meditation have become an integral part of my life, God is also part and parcel of everything. He is no longer 'up there' or 'in church' but with and in me; difficult to describe, but a major change that influences every aspect of living.

It has perhaps encouraged a more tranquil, balanced approach to life. At work I became noted for my calmness in the face of chaos, and my insistence on standing back from problems and taking time to consider, rather than rushing in, knee-jerk fashion. Having developed a knowledge of, or feel for, an inner core of silence and stillness, it seems to spill over into everyday life. It is a well that I can draw on at need, so long as I keep on meditating.

Ideally, JM gives a much wider view of God and our relationship to him and his world than any one church or congregation provides. Certainly, in the groups I have belonged to, people bring such an ecumenical range of experience and reading and insight, we are all enriched and broadened.

Perhaps the sense of equality is why JM seems to appeal to some women? My experience is very limited – but in both groups I have belonged to women far outnumbered men (as they do on the JM advisory group also, and the Church as a whole, of course!).

One other thing JM has given me has been some amazing experiences of God. There have been times when I have 'seen' or experienced aspects of God which have been stunning. I have had to revise my understanding radically, sometimes intellectually, often emotionally as well. Some people have commented that all such experiences 'just come from what you actually think or want but don't recognise'. Since in a number of instances the message I got was highly unwelcome, and at other times astounding in the change of perception demanded, this seems very unlikely. But all have come because I set aside the time and attention to wait on God, and to do so faithfully time and time again, regardless of how 'productive' such sessions seemed to be.

Taking a little church cleaning job thirteen or fourteen years ago has taken me further on my spiritual journey than I would ever have believed – and JM has played a major role in that journey for over half that time.

A celebration of the love of God on Julian's Day

SARAH SALISBURY

We shared silence in the stillness of that beautiful building . . .

In May last year, our Julian Meeting attended the annual Julian

Celebration at Winchester Cathedral. About fifty to sixty people attend and it is held up in the quire in front of the high altar. This is an opportunity for members of Julian Meetings in the Winchester area to meet together to worship, share silence and get to know each other. Our area co-ordinator arranges the date and each year the worship is led by a different Julian Meeting. That evening our JM agreed to lead the service this year.

A year seemed like a long way off, but it was very soon upon us and so, on a beautiful May evening, several car loads of us parked in The Close, in Winchester. We were feeling rather nervous and apprehensive but also very much looking forward to this special opportunity to lead worship at the beautiful cathedral.

Our theme for the evening was based on a reading from Psalm 40:

> I waited, I waited for God, then he stooped to me and heard my cry for help.
> He pulled me up from the seething chasm, from the mud of the mire.
> He set my feet on rock, and made my footsteps firm.
> He put a fresh song in my mouth, praise for our God.
> Many will be awe-struck at the sight, and will put their trust in him.

Our vision was for a large rock to be placed in the centre of our circle of chairs up in the quire of the cathedral. Fortunately the husband of one of our members was able to make us one from papier maché. The rock was set in a mire (black cloth), with a candle with three wicks on the top and covered in small rocks. Members of the congregation were invited to collect a small rock to hold during the silence to focus their prayers on the strength and confidence that comes from God. We chose hymns and wrote prayers on this theme and also had a reading from Julian's own writings, from Chapter 68 of her *Revelations of Divine Love*:

> Just as in his first word that our good Lord revealed, referring to His blessed Passion: "With this is the Devil overcome" – just so He said in this last word with completely true faithfulness, referring to us all: "Thou shalt not be overcome." And all this teaching and this true comfort is universal for all my fellow

> Christians as we said before – and this is God's will. These words: "Thou shalt not be overcome", were said very sharply and very powerfully, for certainty and comfort against all tribulations that can come. He said not: "Thou shalt not be tempted; thou shalt not be troubled; thou shalt not be distressed," but He said, "Thou shalt not be overcome." God wills that we take heed to these words, and that we be very strong in certain trust, in well and in woe, for as He loves and delights in us, so He wills that we love Him and delight in Him and strongly trust in Him; and all shall be well.

The service went well and everyone seemed to enjoy it and receive a feeling of God's strength and peace. We shared silence in the stillness of that beautiful building, bathed in sunlight from the west window, surrounded by stones which had absorbed the prayers of Christians over centuries.

I hope that this article will encourage other groups to consider presenting such an event. We designed the service ourselves, starting with a blank piece of paper and some guidance from Ann Lewin. For all of us it was a first. Twelve of us took part in leading the service itself – it was very much a team effort which did share out the nerves. The service and the preparations beforehand were very special to our group. To lead a service in the cathedral was a great privilege and we have some lovely memories.

The Julian Cell, the Julian Centre, and the Julian Meetings

GRAHAM JOHNSON

Separate organisations, though we do try to assist one another . . .

From time to time members of JM groups visit the Julian Cell and the Julian Centre in Norwich, and sometimes imagine that it is the headquarters of the Julian Meetings. In fact the Julian Centre and the Julian Meetings are two separate organisations, though we do try to assist one another and people often join both.

The Julian Cell is where Julian of Norwich lived and wrote her book *The Revelations of Divine Love*, in a room attached to St Julian's Church in King Street, Norwich. Her hermitage was pulled down later, but it was repaired after wartime bombing. Today pilgrims come from all over the world to kneel in silence and to ponder the words God spoke to her.

The purpose of the cell today is still to be a place of prayer. The worship of the Eucharist and the Divine Office is offered daily in either St Julian's or the nearby parish church and each Friday there is a time of silent intercession. Requests for prayer left by visitors are also offered.

St Julian's Church is tucked away in St Julian's Alley, a small lane which runs between King Street and Rouen Road. From King Street the entrance to the alley is almost opposite Dragon Hall. From Rouen Road (the best approach by car) the alley is beside All Hallows' Hall and the Julian Centre, with the pay-and-display car park opposite. It is a short drive or about ten minutes' walk from Norwich Cathedral.

The Julian Centre is next door to the church, on Rouen Road. Here visitors are welcomed, and cards and books are on sale. There is a reference library that aims to stock everything ever written about Julian, in any language, and a lending library that includes books on general spirituality. Individual visitors and groups are always welcome. Talks on Julian can be arranged on request, and Quiet Days and retreats based at Julian's Cell can be arranged. The Friends of Julian of Norwich receive a regular bulletin and are remembered in prayer on a rota basis by name. Accommodation is often available at the nearby convent, for those wishing to stay near the cell for prayer or study. The address of the Julian Centre is St Julian's Alley, Rouen Road, Norwich, NR1 1QT.

JM spirituality

LIZ TYNDALL

Readers responded to an enquiry in the JM Magazine *of Winter 1995.*

Is there such a thing as Julian spirituality? The answer is 'Yes – most definitely', to quote just one of the people who wrote to me in answer to my article. It has been a fascinating exercise reading the varied responses and discovering a pattern which I think is emerging. 'Spirituality' is a difficult word, for some interpret it as 'the way we pray':

> I hope there isn't such a thing and never will be. Are a lot of different spiritualities really what we want in the Church – especially where they may cause rivalry or one-upmanship? We are all 'even Christians', different people with different gifts, tastes and talents. I am very glad that the Julian Meetings did decide against a common membership and a specific rule years ago.

So am I. And so, I think, are the rest of you. For the picture that emerges is one of enormous variation characterised by a breadth, depth, flexibility, openness and acceptance that is hard to find elsewhere, and that we seem to experience as a true movement of the spirit for our times. This may be what Martin Israel sensed when he spoke of what we have to offer to the peace of the world. And it is this that I would like to explore under the blanket term of 'spirituality'.

A feminine spirituality

> As I read through *Circles of Silence*, I can't think of any other source which could have produced articles of such depth and scope and all related in some way to the centrality of contemplative prayer. I think that it is perhaps a fundamental openness, and I would see it as essentially feminine – open to the growth and evolution of experience and ideas, as they emerge from lived experience.

Some have maintained in the past that contemplative prayer is the female expression within the Yin and Yang of the life of prayer. But this correspondent compares the styles of different teachers of meditation, citing the Guru-led John Main school, with its hierarchical structure, its specific teaching and emphasis on form, as 'masculine'. By contrast she writes:

> JM says, "This is how it can be done . . . or this . . . or this . . . whatever is right for you . . . and this is what my practice has led me to." It's altogether more organic, and therefore more creative, open to the unexpected, the new. So I would see JM spirituality as open to the new, yet centred in a long tradition of experience of others who have also been open to the new. It's a spirituality which is quiet yet vibrant . . . perhaps the analogy of the child in the womb . . . a very feminine spirituality.

Does this mean that men who are happy in JM are those who are on good terms with the feminine in their own nature? Another correspondent writes of the feminine: 'Certainly not a passive spirituality, but one that is most active and challenging. As indeed the legacy of Julian should be!'

In a very real sense there is nothing new in our spirituality. People of prayer have been here before us and have much to show us. But we are here, and now, and can begin to recognise the new thing that God is doing in and through us. It is not our way to proclaim it from the housetops. But we are now of age. Perhaps as we grow into maturity we should become more visible.

Growth

As a seed sown secretly develops and grows almost unnoticed, so JM has an influence on individuals and also on the wider Church and community. Little groups, so often of those perceived as the least important in the wider Church, discovering the prayer of the heart in their own communities, are moving mountains. This prayer has always been around, but usually locked up in convents or bishops' palaces. The message of JM (as with other contemplative groups) is that we can all be part of this transforming power, whatever our age, sex, denomination, churchmanship, intelligence and physical ability, however weak our faith – just so long as we wish to learn about Christ-centred meditation. And then we change individually to:

A more open and mature spirituality.

Added depth.

Learning to be quiet, but in one's own way . . . to find God in silence (at least free from words) . . . to wait and listen . . . to feel his wishes and his power.

All that has been accomplished, all that has been aimed for, has been inspired by the ability to approach God in quiet contemplation. This approach becomes easier, more instant as confidence grows, and this confidence is perhaps the greatest gift I have received from the Julian Meetings.

There really hasn't been any influence in my life to compare with JM. It has been a dominant factor in everything I have been able to achieve within the church and beyond. And I feel that the ability to approach God and call on his strength is the greatest gift I have received.

I think that being a Julian has very much affected my whole approach to life. I see now that I always needed it, especially when bringing up a family and I simply didn't know of anything of the sort . . . My husband and I meditate together morning and evening and I think this strengthens our relationships and helps us to work out our priorities. I know I'm calmer and much more prepared to accept what will be without struggling.

Circles of silence

Our book was aptly named. The power of JM lies in the mushrooming growth of small groups. And it often lies in their apparent weakness. We have sometimes been tempted in the Advisory Group to try to produce a blueprint, or at the least 'guidelines' . . . in fact we have done that! But basically each group functions autonomously and does its own thing. Some talk more, some less, some come and go in silence. Some drink coffee, some don't. Some are very small and meet often, sharing a lot. Others are large and more formal. Some fail, but most don't, at least until they have served their turn. In most groups the humanity is important, especially for uncertain newcomers. There is a sense of being upheld, of being safe and of being able to talk about the most intimate things in safety . . . even prayer and failure! Despite this openness, this depth of sharing, JM groups have maintained their openness to newcomers, their 'flexible attendance so that the group does not become a cosy clique'. I think this is a feature of many groups, and it implies a rare form of trust.

JM has always had an open structure and welcomes members of all faiths and none. Ideally we leave our creeds and our learnt assumptions at the door so that we may meet with people as people and with God as God. Sometimes we do actually 'take the shoes off our feet' – for comfort? or because we sense that we are on holy ground? And as we leave words behind and enter the world of symbols our minds and hearts click into a more open, more receptive frame. Some people may be able to do this alone, but for most of us (especially when we start) the accepting group is essential – the yardstick against which we can test our own experience. And it always remains valuable. Some already have an experience of silence and may have been confused, even scared by it:

> I was already into contemplative prayer although I didn't know what I was doing. I was in a kind of dark night/wilderness in which no regular form of prayer or church practice made any kind of sense. I just sat beside (my dying husband) and waited.

This correspondent goes on to show how her experience of a Julian Meeting group helped her through the death and into a totally new lifestyle. Another puts it this way:

> All I know of spirituality has come from JM. These are the main points which come to mind. (i) Warmth and strength of the prayer together. (ii) Feeling of oneness with those one meets and prays with regularly. Giving a background of support to one's prayer life. (iii) Praying with people who would not be found in the church of one's choice. Across a divide which is man-made, prayers can be offered in unity. (iv) Friendships – depth of experience – giving and receiving. (v) Private prayer is strengthened by the knowledge of the praying of others.

And another, disarmingly, probably speaks for many of us:

> I realise that being silent is only the beginning and that "letting go" will eventually lead to a real inner stillness, but I am very bad at this personally.

Our freedom from rules allows us to be where we are, now, and relieves us from that sense of guilt which dogs the prayer of so many sincere God-lovers.

A final comment may sum up for many of us what we would like to say of our own experience of Julian Meetings:

> The meetings I attended were very positive instances of prayer followed by contemplative silence. One could sense the full "engagement" of those present. Each one of us returns to "reality" refreshed, invigorated and encouraged to express more openly that divine love we have touched in the deep well of silence.

Going beyond

There is one felt need, expressed by several writers, which JM in general is not addressing sufficiently – that of teaching. There is a problem here, for contemplation is the subject matter, above all others, that we grasp only when we are personally ready for it. So I pass the questions back: should there be more teaching in our groups? – and if so, how? Do the groups each have a lending library? Do people use it?

Once I thought that JM would have a short life before being absorbed back into the local churches who would by then have accepted the need for everyone to experience a little of silence in prayer and worship. This is not going to happen yet! And we must be very wary of becoming a sort of alternative church, for that will only marginalise us and cut the message off from the wider body of Christ. Perhaps we should just continue to grow secretly. Or it may be that, with our Coming of Age, the time has come to go public and to claim aloud for God what he has been doing among us, in terms of restoring, renewing and revitalising our individual and corporate life. But we must beware. One such warning was expressed like this:

> There is the danger of the 'establishmentising' of JM . . . The new thing that God does is always outside of known boundaries, and whilst as humans we need boundaries as both support and discipline and yardsticks for the ego, nevertheless they are only to be transcended in God's good time. As Father Bede Griffiths used to say: "We must always go beyond".

I would like to end with another quotation from another visionary of the world-wide Church who has experienced disillusionment, suffering and silence. Jurgen Moltmann writes of his hope for the future, calling it 'congregation' (which means simply those who meet together):

> "Congregation" is a new kind of living together for human beings that affirms:
> that no one is alone with his or her own problems;
> that no one has to conceal his or her own disabilities;
> and that there are not some who have the say and others who have nothing to say;
> that neither the old nor the little ones are isolated;
> that the one bears the other even when it is unpleasant and there is no agreement;
> and that, finally, the one can also at times leave the other in peace when the other needs it.
> This is the new temple of Christ which calls for our whole attention.

Is this the 'beyond' to which the silence of God is drawing us, in the van of his Church?

The spirituality of Julian Meetings and other contemplative networks

HEBE WELBOURN

> *All the groups practise the prayer of quiet, listening and being, as opposed to talking, singing or using the imagination.*

As warden of a house of contemplative prayer I thought I would compile resource information on the different contemplative prayer networks. I already knew about Julian Meetings because I had been a member for several years. My house had been founded by Elsie Briggs who was instrumental in starting Julian Meetings in Bristol and two groups were already meeting here when I moved in. I wrote to the National Retreat Association for their Christian Contemplative Meditation Groups list, which is produced annually for them by Michael Tiley, a member of the JM advisory group. These included five groups in addition to JM: The Christian Meditation Centre (John Main Trust), the Fellowship of Contemplative Prayer, Contemplative Prayer (Carmelite), the Fellowship of Meditation, and Servants of Christ the King. I also contacted Christian TM, and Contemplative Outreach UK (Centring Prayer based on the teaching of Fr Thomas Keating, a Cistercian) and I attend the Society of Friends and the Bristol Ch'an (Zen Buddhist) Group. I have explored the Orthodox tradition to the extent that my personal practice is based on the Jesus Prayer, and I use icons – as do many other contemplatives in JM and other settings. How do I find the 'Spirituality of JM' in relation to all these other groups?

I must emphasise that what I have written is personal – what I find. Participants of JM or one of the other networks may feel that what I have written is inaccurate or not true. For instance I describe JM as 'Anglican' and 'English' – this is not a statement of objective fact (JM is actually very ecumenical and eclectic), but reflects what I find. As someone with roots in the Anglican Church and English culture and countryside, I feel particularly at home in JM. The exploration of silence will inevitably lead some people deeply into the mystical wilderness where guidance and discipline will be necessary. I, personally, have been helped by membership of a Ch'an (Zen) Buddhist group. Also, I have worked as a doctor and have been engaged in psychotherapy. The things I notice and the way I describe them are inevitably coloured by my personal experience. Others might find different aspects, but my findings may still be of interest to them.

All the groups practise the prayer of quiet, listening and being, as opposed to talking, singing or using the imagination. Some forms of Christian meditation use the imagination – notably Ignatian prayer – and this overlaps with other eastern and western meditation techniques which may be part of the experience of any contemplative Christian these days, but are not actually contemplative, i.e., silent, still, centred. The Society of Friends and the Servants of Christ the King (which I will not refer to again) enter silence in a slightly different way. There may be a very deep quality of silence, but there is a waiting upon the Spirit and at any time a member of the meeting may be moved to speech. This overlaps towards the experience of charismatic prayer groups where the Spirit breaks through very exuberantly and members may fall about or speak with tongues. The Spirit at work in a contemplative prayer group leads more deeply into silence and one-pointed awareness.

This leads to the question of spiritual gifts in prayer. In Buddhist and other established meditation practices one seeks an experience of changed consciousness or enlightenment. In Christian meditation these gifts may occur but they are not sought for their own sake. The same may be said of charismatic gifts, tongues, Toronto blessing, miracles – they may occur but are not sought. The same applies to healing, psychotherapy, pain relief, stress relief – all may occur but are not sought. All the main Christian meditation networks set out to help ordinary, lay Christians into the prayer of silence. They all agree that we may find ourselves quietly changed – perhaps a greater abundance of the fruits of the Spirit: love, joy, peace, endurance, etc.

The gift sometimes sought by meditators is the ability to zonk at will into a state of light trance. This is a gift which has its uses, but is not essential to contemplative prayer. In Julian Meetings there is no expectation of trance: most people have difficulty in describing what happens during the silence; for some it seems that most of the time is spent just sitting quietly among the distractions. Christian Meditation Centre practice, on the other hand, is derived from yogic experience and some of their teachers suggest the desirability of a state of trance with very slowed down respiration and pulse rates, etc. Profoundly altered consciousness may be accompanied by other experiences: visualisations, bliss, out of body experiences, etc. People with 'psychic gifts' or psychiatric instability may run into trouble. We badly need directors steeped in Christian tradition who are at home in this border-country of spiritual experience. Meanwhile, Julian Meetings, being very homely and ordinary are seldom called upon to engage in this area.

Most of the groups are based on the experience of leaders who have received instruction in eastern (Buddhist or Hindu) meditation practices. It might be expected that there would be network support for contemplative groups extending from contemplative religious communities and their oblates, but this happens mainly on an individual basis. Exceptions to this are groups based on two outstanding individual teachers: Fr Matthew McGetrick, a Carmelite, and Fr

Thomas Keating, an American Cistercian – both authors of best-selling books. Fr Matthew was a saintly man who died recently. Fr Thomas Keating's teaching was extended in this country via a network called Contemplative Outreach, but his teaching does not really transmit without his presence. We could certainly do with other teachers gifted with the ability to transmit traditional Christian contemplative experience at a deep level.

John Main was a Benedictine monk who learned meditation from an Indian swami while working for the colonial service in Malaysia. He has died but his teaching survives on tape and in the person of Laurence Freeman in the Christian Meditation Centre (CMC).

The Fellowship of Contemplative Prayer (FCP) was started by an Anglican priest, Robert Coulson, in 1946. He was born in Russia, lived in Estonia and moved to England with the Revolution. Between the wars, he was influenced by Marian Dunlop, the founder of the Fellowship of Meditation. He developed a spiritual theology which is the basis of their teaching. He died in December 1995, but the work is carried on by the Revd Martin Tunnicliffe, the secretary, and a team of trustees and other volunteers.

The Fellowship of Meditation (FM) was founded by Marian Dunlop in 1932. She was introduced to meditation in about 1908, by attending lectures in meditation and healing by a pioneer American psychologist, Dr Porter Mills. She evolved a practice of meditation and healing linked with the Guild of Health. She died in 1974, but her teaching is continued by her successors based on her house in Dorchester.

All three of these networks use a discipline of meditation based on holy words. John Main recommends the use of a single word (mantra) such as 'maranatha' ('Come, Lord Jesus') as a focus for attention. A basic discipline of daily twenty minutes' meditation with a mantra is recommended. Training for leaders is provided by means of audio-visual aids, retreats and regional Quiet Days led by Fr Laurence Freeman and members of the whole-time staff team.

The FCP and FM use biblical texts as a starting point for silent meditation. In both cases membership is based on a rule of daily meditation using the sacred text, as taught by the founder. The FCP lays great emphasis on the 'Dominical' ('I am') sayings of Jesus as particular means of receiving the Holy Spirit. Group leaders and retreat leaders are trained by means of networking and retreats. Meetings are structured with words used as a basis for shortish periods of silence. There is a regular retreat, a newsletter and a council of trustees, most of whom knew the founder personally. The FM also has a rule, membership and training retreats. All three are committed to training in a discipline according to a method initiated by their founder.

The CMC is endowed with property in London and Canada and has a whole-time headquarters staff. The FM also possesses a house and a whole-time secretary. The FCP has a highly committed part-time leadership team, including two who live in houses of prayer.

When the Julian Meetings were started, in 1973, Hilary Wakeman was responding to the need which we still feel for a contemplative base in our busy churches. She wrote to the Church newspapers of all the main denominations and had an overwhelming response. She herself is Anglican, as also were her supporters after the first year, the Cowley Fathers. But from the outset members have been drawn from all churches, and some have no church membership. Leadership has always been informal and non-clerical. There are no teachers and no trainees. There is no structure, no rule of life and no permanent headquarters.

All the networks are, in principle, ecumenical. The CMC is a Roman Catholic foundation, but welcomes members from any denomination. The FCP is an Anglican initiative but is ecumenical. JM in England has an Anglican majority but denominational allegiance is never referred to. The celebration of the Eucharist in an ecumenical setting sadly continues to be a problem. However 'open' the intention there are likely to be some who feel excluded – not least Quakers. At retreats, JM celebrates a kind of 'shadow' eucharistic liturgy using an empty chalice and paten (known as the 'Eucharist of the Heart'). This is a powerful, silent expression of the pain of drawing close to each other while remaining separated. This powerful experience is part of the essence of 'JM spirituality'.

There is also the inter-faith dimension. Many Christians turn to contemplative prayer because they experience trauma or irrelevance among the external structures of church life. Some turn to Buddhist or New Age styles of meditation: we shop around and become fragmented. There is a heady sense of freedom from clichés for a Christian meditating in a Buddhist setting – after a while, though, one comes to appreciate that even Buddhists have their religious 'guff'. In silence we can tune in together to our deep underlying harmony. The silence can also be a comfortable muffler. Contemplative prayer will, if we are honest, lead us into the border country of our faith (if we are not already there when we start). If we are to survive and be honest, we need to test our boundaries, try to talk about our structures and differences while maintaining some kind of a link with a centre. The Roman Catholic leadership of the CMC handles this area with experienced subtlety, smoothing the way for 'good Catholic' meditators. JM, in 'good Anglican' fashion, accommodates itself to a wide variety of methods without talking about it much. Whoever we are, we need spiritual companionship, direction and a tap root to a central tradition.

How, then, would I summarise 'JM spirituality' in this context? First it is not only 'Anglican' but also very 'English'. There is no provision for instruction in eastern-style meditation, no central authority and a minimum of structure. It is democratic. There is no rule of life or system of training of leaders. The purpose of the group is silence and there is a minimum of verbal sharing. It is okay for a group member to sleep: God works in us in sleep as well as in awareness. There is a temptation for a group to become too cosy and relaxed and miss the vocation to watchful awareness. There is a need for watchful, prophetic 'subversive contemplatives'. There is a need for guidance within the Christian tradition for contemplatives exploring a mystical path. Having said this, JM through its magazine and pamphlets provides really excellent basic resource material for ordinary or fringe Christians, and at most Julian Group Meetings and retreats you will find a deep level of shared silence.

Note: It has been pointed out to me that what I wrote about the World Community for Christian Meditation and the Christian Meditation Centre, is open to misunderstanding. CM practice is based on the teaching of John Main who learned meditation with a mantra in the East, and found the same in a Christian tradition – notably with John Cassian and *The Cloud of Unknowing* – meditation with a Christian mantra.

When we come to talk about our experiences in altered states of consciousness we run into trouble. A Christian may talk cheerfully of having had a wonderful night's sleep: we recognise that the Lord provides for his beloved while they sleep (Psalm 127). Some Christians will talk about being drawn very deeply into prayer, deeply centred, deeply relaxed – a condition in which bodily activity (pulse, respiration, brain activity) will be slowed down. Of course, these physical changes are quite ordinary, they don't matter. No one suggests they should be sought as ends in themselves.

Twenty-first-century JM

HILARY WAKEMAN

> *As someone involved with JM from the very beginning I think I can say that the ethos of JM is largely covered by the word 'simplicity'.*

Where is JM going? And how can we ensure that, rather than being directed by our own very human inclinations, we are allowing the Spirit of God to lead us? The Julian Meetings have been in existence for twenty-eight years and it seemed to the Advisory Group that it was time for an evaluation of some sort.

Having a minimum of organisation is part of the Julian Meetings' ethos. There are no paid staff, no office premises, and no boards or committees other than the minimalist Advisory Group. Each of its ten members has a task, and the group meets two and a half times a year to share information and make any necessary decisions. The 'half a meeting' is a couple of hours at the end of the annual JM-UK retreat, and the other two consist of a day meeting in London, and a residential weekend in May at a retreat house. Although that May weekend is normally part informal retreat and part business, this year's was different.

We met at The Grail, in Pinner on the outskirts of London. To lead us in our thinking we had Sister Madeleine Prendergast SUSC. Madeleine is wise and holy and worldly, affectionate and sharp-witted. We could not have had a better facilitator.

First she had us considering the strengths of JM. We listed many factors. Then separately, but unanimously, we came up with two that seemed important above all the others:

- JM is about a yearning for God;
- it is ecumenical.

After that, we looked at what might 'break in, steal and destroy' the strengths we had identified. Among other factors we recognised that:

- our Anglican majority could be a problem if it led us to unthinking assumptions;
- there may be a danger of self-aggrandisement, as in the matter of publicity for JM: is it for the Kingdom – or for ourselves?

- the very freedom of JM, which is so valued, could lead to some local Meetings deviating from the JM ethos by being too structured, or built on individual power-trips, or not based on silence, or having no intention of being ecumenical (the same could be true of JM in other countries).

And finally, in the light of these strengths and threats, we looked to what needs attention in the future. The most important points seemed to be:

- inclusivity: we need to ensure a good age spread in the Advisory Group and to encourage the same in individual Meetings;
- promotion: we reminded ourselves that from the very start, the teaching and enabling of contemplative prayer has been the purpose of JM, and that we should be encouraging more teaching;
- organisation: we felt that Advisory Group members could be more aware that a growing organisation means a growing burden of work, that should be recognised and then shared evenly; also, that links between the Advisory Group and individual Meetings could be improved; and that we should recognise that 'belonging' to JM was important to people.

Again and again the phrase 'JM ethos' came up, and Sr Madeleine had us look at that in some depth by explaining it to her. Doing that, we realised that what is taken for granted by some long-term 'Julians' is unknown history to newer ones. And that it might be useful to say something about it now, for the benefit of twenty-first-century JM.

As someone who has been involved with JM from the very beginning, I think I can say that the ethos of JM is largely covered by the word 'simplicity'. It involves minimal structures, no rules or regulations, no 'gurus', no distinction between clergy and lay people, and no hierarchy in the local Meetings or in the Advisory Group. We have no 'rule of life' or doctrinal requirements, and we advocate no specific meditation techniques or mantras. We ask only that Meetings be based on contemplative prayer, in the Christian tradition, and be at least potentially ecumenical.

Some examples of this ethos:

- After a few years as numbers and correspondence grew, we experimented with paying an honorarium to the convenor. But somehow we felt it spoiled participants' relationship with the convenor and the practice was dropped. Instead, the work was shared out among the members of the Advisory Group, which then grew with the work.

- It was once suggested that we register as a charity, to enable us to accept a donation from another charity. When we discovered this would require us to draw up a Constitution, and have an AGM and an Annual Report, we decided against it. (Our accounts have, of course, always been available to anyone who wishes to see them.)
- Some years ago when a well-known religious order was considering disposing of one of its houses, the Advisory Group was invited to say what its response would be if the house was offered to JM. Briefly we agonised over it, then concluded that owning property would tie us down, and would therefore be a wrong move.

It was good that we did this evaluation at this time. Thanks to Sr Madeleine's skilful guidance we came away from our exploration with some confidence that JM continues to fulfil a need – and is still open to being guided by God.

Screwtape alive and well

GRAHAM JOHNSON

In 1997 the editorship of the Julian Meetings Magazine *changed hands, and the following piece was written by the new editor. At first glance it is a book review . . .*

The Noise Fights Back by A. Tony de Malo (Inferno Press), 750 pages.

This book is a response to *Circles of Silence*, the anthology of articles from the *Julian Meetings Magazine* collected together during the time Pamela Fawcett was editor. Where possible, the editor of *The Noise Fights Back* has grouped his contributions under the major heading of 'Distractions'. Space does not permit a list of all these (the index alone is 250 pages) but a glance at the contents shows that several pages are given over to 'Organisation' where the subheadings are:

(1) 'Meetings and literature to promote a tight structure at contemplative prayer meetings'. This includes ensuring that everyone thinks and prays the same way (though I note that this is contradicted on page 109 in sub-section 4(ii) which encourages people who snore or criss-cross their legs during the silence, and on page 234 which tells you how to annoy/be the envy of the rest of your group by detailing the wonderful visions you had during the silence).
(2) 'Listing penalties for Group Secretaries who do not send in details of their group in time'.
(3) 'Devising more and more spiritual literature to make contemplation appear difficult or "much too holy for me" '.
(4) 'Preparing a book of choruses to be sung at group meetings'. The editor suggests that this has a treble purpose. Not only is time wasted on preparing the book of choruses, and not only does it make JM Meetings noisy affairs, but it leads to arguments within the group as to which tune should be sung and at what speed.
(5) 'Choosing a leader'. The editor is concerned to deprive a group of its full potential by the 'choosing' (by which he means someone pushing himself forward) of one person who always leads and tells the others what to do.

Other chapter headings include 'Fears and Worries'. Here the editor is keen to play on people's fear of other denominations and religions. In the resources section of the book there are addresses for the manufacturers of blinkers, and T-shirts with the legend 'If the *Book of Common Prayer* was good enough for Jesus . . . '

The final chapter is entitled 'In the last resort'. This deals with what 'The Noise' must do if it discovers the perfect Julian Meeting in which the members are truly open to God in the silence and to one another. Here the recommendation is to ensure that this divine energy is kept bound up within the group so preventing an overflow into social concern and direct prophetic action like damaging Hawk bombers, harbouring illegal immigrants, supporting gay liberation, or tunnelling under prospective runways.

Being perfect myself and not prone to any of the above temptations, I cannot recommend this book but I am sure that it will be a bestseller. All the more reason then to ensure that we sell more and more copies of *Circles of Silence* and encourage more and more people in our Julian Meetings to buy their own copy of the *JM Magazine*, which for so long, and especially under Pamela's editorship, has prepared people for the times when the Noise fights back.

SECTION EIGHT

'The opportunity to let God be God': retreats and Quiet Days

Leaf prayer

About 130 Julian Meetings sent in prayers written on a leaf symbol for the annual retreat in 1999. This one is from Poringland in Norfolk.

In the silence challenge us, but give us your peace.
In the silence activate us, but give us your rest.
In the silence hold us close to your heart and give us your blessing.

Impressions of a first retreat

CAROL PUNCHON

I went with an open mind, but hoping to find peace . . .

As we arrived at Launde Abbey the words of the twenty-third Psalm sprang into my mind and stayed with me throughout the weekend. It is in a very peaceful spot surrounded by gentle rolling hills. Sheep come and graze in the spacious grounds.

There was an atmosphere of stillness and silence in the house. The accommodation was comfortable, the food was good. A large part of our weekend was spent in small groups. We experienced different 'lead-ins' and plenty of restful silence. I didn't feel the need to know details about the lives of other members. They are irrelevant in a group experience of silence. The silence, the 'waiting on the Spirit', brought a feeling of intimacy and unity.

The weekend was blessed with mild and sunny weather. On Saturday afternoon I joined in the circle dancing session on the lawn and then experienced an awareness walk. The Sunday morning Eucharist of the Heart reminded us of the pain of disunity but also the hope to come when we will all gather at one table. The service included a thoughtful address on angels and some of the visual symbols were moving – the empty chalice and paten, the paintings placed around the altar and the pools of colour cast on the floor by the sun shining through the stained glass windows.

This was my first Julian retreat, so I went with an open mind, but hoping to find peace and rest. I was not disappointed. By the time I left I had been led by still waters and my soul was restored.

Reflections on a JM retreat

DIANA MILLS

If we act as Christ's living cells, then through us Christ is alive.

Among the many inspired instances of silent and spoken sharing during our national JM weekend at Launde Abbey two key points stand out in my mind: cells, and contemplation in action. Together they form what could be described as a 'dynamic duo' that illustrates clearly what Julian's spiritual legacy is all about.

Granted this is a personal interpretation. I have no doubt others will have discovered different and equally valid aspects. For what my own reflections may be worth, I'd like to share them by beginning with the key point of cells.

During our circles of silence I found myself thinking about the analogy of the hazelnut that appears in Chapter 5 of Julian's *Revelations*: something so small and vulnerable, yet it contains the whole of God's creation within itself because, as Julian writes, 'God loves it'. This is a tremendously moving and powerful image. Creation is not a one-off event that happened at a specific point in linear time and will never take place again. It is a continual, and ongoing process arising from the urge of God's will to create and God's love which brings that will into existence. Imagine the concentrated energy of divine will and love working unceasingly within that single hazelnut as it lies, embryo-like, within the womb formed by the cup of Julian's hand!

In reflecting more deeply on the hazelnut as a single cell of creation within the boundless expanse of space, I saw each one of us as individual cells linked together by the wonder of 'waiting on God' in loving stillness. Yet a cell that waits is by no means purely passive, nor is the waiting a completely negative action. There is an active aspect, which is the contribution we as individual cells make to the community in response to inspiration received during that stillness.

Groupings of like-motivated cells give life to the community to which they belong, while the community itself is a larger cell within an ever-widening circle. Thus, following a harmonious pattern of interaction from cells to communities to circles, we build up the Body of Christ. For in essence this is what we are: living cells of a divine, universal Body, the vital fabric of its very blood, bone and marrow. If we act as Christ's living cells, then through us Christ is alive. Without those living cells to sustain it the Body will die.

Our responsibility for keeping Christ alive in the world is far greater than perhaps we even dare imagine.

These reflections bring me to the second key point, that of contemplation in action.

Contemplation entails being open to God, not for any personal message regarding our spiritual efforts, but in order to understand to the best of our human ability what it is that God desires us to do for others. How can we, as cells of the living Christ, best serve God's purpose for the world in which we find ourselves at a given time? That world may be our family, our church or our community. It may be circumscribed by our personal relationships. It may extend to the far corners of the earth. We never know when or how God is going to call on us, nor where our response may lead us. We can only tune our minds and hearts to the voice of God, listening attentively in the depths of our inner silence.

The Gospels provide us with a perfect example of this. Whenever Christ needed to communicate with God he withdrew from his disciples and the eager crowd of his followers to a place where he could be alone in peace and silence. These periods of contemplation were followed by heightened ministry and deeper spiritual insight, as though his batteries had been recharged with the endless energy of God's love.

Returning from the peace and beauty of Launde Abbey, we bring with us that same energy which has been given to each one according to our individual needs and capabilities. It is, of course, not always easy to find the time, let alone the space, for even a minute of silence to listen to God. Yet when the will truly exists, the way is provided. We need to learn how to recognise this when it happens and to use that moment to its fullest. Gradually, as we build up confidence in our own awareness, we learn how to withdraw into that inner space of silence while carrying on with our external tasks. In this way contemplation and action are no longer separate processes. They have become interactive and in so doing strengthen each other.

At Launde Abbey we waited together on God in our circles of silence; together we broke silence and as a community discussed the way forward. Now, as living cells of Christ, we re-enter our daily lives to translate into positive action everything we have shared and learned from each other so that the Body of which we are a part may increase in the fullness of grace and truth.

A Quiet Day in a garden

DAMIEN CULSHAW

I came to realise that we have a great worth without action.

Imagine the scene – a warm sun, the sky a vivid blue, trees and grass in new summer green, a gentle breeze rustling the leaves and stroking the skin. Time stood still, all worries and activity aside; a great sense of being and belonging.

Good news! The garden is close by. It could be your own garden or a scene during a country walk or even your own bedroom; appreciation of the garden is mostly an attitude of mind. In our case the garden was that of a Christian soul from Childrey who loaned theirs to the 'Julian' and 'Wellsprings' groups last Saturday.

In case I have lost you completely . . . These groups are quiet meditation groups led by a Wantage Sister who works at St Katherine's House. Julian was Julian of Norwich, and Wellsprings water the garden I suppose (I am not very advanced yet). The church noticeboard says that Wellsprings is a guided meditation group, based on Anthony de Mello's books *Sadhana* (Garden City, 1986) and *Wellsprings* (Garden City, 1984).

At Wellsprings what we have been gently encouraged to practise are prayer exercises which stop us judging, analysing, and generally busying our minds with clutter. This is in fact very difficult to do even (especially) when we are trying to pray. The idea is that you stop chattering and just sit still, quietening your mind. This is made easier by concentrating on one thing at a time – for example your breathing. Up until now reaching some degree of quiet for a few minutes has been all I have been able to manage.

The 'Quiet Day' we enjoyed last Saturday was the first time that I was able to really enjoy some of what God is offering in the silence. There were few rules on the day – we could wander around the garden or the village at will but we were not allowed to speak until the 3 p.m. sharing session – even during lunch (I allowed myself a smile as I returned a tennis ball to a lad who had been playing exuberantly on a court next door). We started in the morning with the quietening exercises we had become used to in the monthly sessions. We were then set free to walk. We were encouraged to take our time and tune into each of our senses in turn.

We were asked to bring something with us to the sharing session, even objects. I brought a feather because I had so much enjoyed rediscovering the sense of touch: cool leaves, prickly grass, soft, tickly feather. I say 'rediscovered' because I remembered this Garden of Eden sensation from childhood. It was a sense of allowing yourself to be rather than do. I came to realise that our value is not just our output, our doing, but that we have a great worth without action.

I found myself enjoying a large old tree which just stood there in the middle of the garden. I watched it just being there, realising that it had done that for a hundred years and I loved it for what it was. God had been feeding it with air and water and occasionally rustling its leaves with a gentle breeze. I realised that we too have the same quality.

The dead tree in High Leigh garden

HEBE WELBOURN

If it is so difficult to convey the experience of a tree, how about God?

I spent nearly an hour (during the retreat) walking around the dead tree, relating to it as I would to an abstract sculpture. My attention was directed to it when I noticed someone drawing. She told me afterwards she wanted to draw the animals in it. I had also seen the animals. But, this time, I was not going to be distracted by imagining animal forms. I wanted to relate to the tree in itself. It seemed very old. Dead, but with a few small twigs showing signs of recent buds. The main trunk was greyish green, warm to the touch, horizontally ridged and pitted with wormholes. Just above my head the trunk divided into two branches and these divided into limbs which grew back, interweaved, and even fused in some places to produce the most intricate multi-dimensional pattern. The pattern had been reduced to its essentials by skilful pruning which had removed all the small growth with the exception of the few twigs.

How to hold this tree in my mind? How to communicate it to others or file it for my own future reference? A photograph? A one-dimensional image, even lots and lots of views from different positions, might make interesting pictures, but they would not be the tree. A video? This would convey something of the moving pattern I experienced as I walked round and changed my viewpoint, but could not convey multi-dimensional solidity. Nor would it convey change over time. If a video camera had been placed beside the tree for a hundred or so years and then played back over a period of ten minutes, we could have seen the tree changing. Although apparently still, it is continually changing. In old age (like me) it experiences decay rather than growth, and this is beautiful too. And all this fails to take into account the continually changing pattern of colour as the sun comes and goes in the clouds, or the moon by night. Sometimes the pattern is light against dark, sometimes dark against bright sky, and it is surrounded by brilliant greens and purple shadows.

Could I draw it, paint it, or make a sculpture? No. My consciousness cannot hold even this simplified unit of complexity as a whole. What about a computer? An infinite number of digital points in time and space. Even a computer has difficulty in coping with what happens beyond infinity, or even in what may happen tomorrow – though I suppose even that can be expressed in terms of an infinite number of possibilities. And having got my computerised image, I can only relate to it in terms of what can be displayed on my VDU. I can write about it, or write a poem. Can I, in some small way, convey awe, delight, interaction? Has the presence of the tree in some way been enhanced by the many as well as myself who have appreciated it?

If it is so difficult to convey the experience of a tree, how about God? We cannot hold anything – not even Transfiguration. All must go into silence. But after a few moments of silence, I want to tell you about it. That's earth for you! And it's also something about what we try to do when we preach the gospel.

Holding fast

FIONA WALLACE

To give ourselves is everything.

Wanda Nash introduced JM-UK's 1996 annual retreat using a quotation from Julian's *Revelations of Divine Love*: 'Perceive it, receive it, hold fast to it', the 'it' being the 'I AM' of God. The 'I AM' indicates that God is with us now, no matter who we are, or the circumstances we are in. God is now, this very instant.

To 'perceive' this we need to be open to God, just as we are. We need no preparation, just the anticipation of a little space and time to share with God. We need not offer anything, or have any expectations, but to 'be'. To give ourselves is everything.

'Receiving' happens in the waiting, in the being, in the sharing with God. Sometimes we may not know that we are receiving, for it is God working in us. We are gently absorbing all that is God into ourselves. We can let go of intercessional prayers and offer these to God to enable us to enter directly into God the Trinity, becoming at one with him. In embracing God, the Son and the Spirit, the Trinity undoubtedly embraces us – 'rest in me and I rest in you'.

An additional aspect Wanda gave us was of 'merriment'. This gave an insight into how God delights in us now for who we are – not who we seem to be to others or even to ourselves, but for who we really are, deep, deep inside at our very core. This core is the part of us which God wills us to explore – where we have talent and love and so much to give. Everyone has this gift, and through knowing the 'I am' of God, it can be discovered.

Finally, 'holding fast to it' can only be achieved by continuing this one-ness with God, by offering ourselves just as we are. Jesus gave us examples of this in many ways. As Wanda put it: 'Every thought, emotion and action was underpinned by his communion with his Father'. Jesus also 'held fast to it' by frequently withdrawing from people, and all expectations, to be alone with God. The expectations put upon Jesus may have been beyond his reaching at that moment, but he acknowledged this, then deflected these expectations to be 're-tuned to the glory of God'. In this way, his own 'being-ness' could remain complete and whole, maintaining his own selfhood. He also coped by creating for himself his own support group. God works in all of us and Jesus wisely used this resource. Jesus knew he was totally loved, totally delighted in by God, and he showed this delight generously towards those in need, knowing it was inexhaustible but respecting his own exhaustibility.

The retreat presented us with the wonderful insight that we may be encouraged by God, Jesus and the Spirit, now! We saw how the Spirit works in and through us as we perceive and receive; how we may delight in the merriment of surrounding love and goodness; how we may take heart as we feel over burdened – for the pressures on Jesus must have been unimaginable, yet he coped, by 'holding fast to it'. All God asks of us is that we might stay with him for just a little while, just as we are, to share in the moment of now-ness. 'I am,' he calls, 'now. I am here, loving you now, for I am God.'

A wordsmith's paradoxical contribution to silence

JIM COTTER

> *So many of the words we use in public prayer have lost their power to connect. So we wander off in our own silences . . .*

What on earth is a wordsmith doing leading a retreat for those whose way of prayer leaves words behind and enters an ever-deepening silence?

Well, it is a puzzle but let me explore it. I do not think that words and silence are bound to be in opposition, nor that they need be kept in two compartments. Unfortunately, this is the usual impression in most acts of worship. Silence is used to cover movement, or it falls into a gap because somebody has missed a cue. Or, following many words, there is the bidding, 'Let us keep silence for a minute or two.' (This invariably means twenty seconds at most.) Then we are back to the words. We get on with the real thing. One such silence was punctuated by the stage whispers of an elderly woman in the congregation, 'Is something wrong?', and a minute later, 'Is it time to go home?'

Surely words and silence can be more closely connected. Think of the silence of breathing in at leisure, and of a word taking shape as we breathe out: the word is 'carried' on the breath, larynx and lips helping it on its way. Think of poetry well spoken, in which pauses are an integral part of the reading, allowing the imagination room to move, enhancing the meaning, and leading easily and almost inevitably into silence. Or think of the silence out of which new unfoldings of the truth emerge precisely because the silence itself has purged much of the chatter that usually fills our conversations, both inner and outer.

So we may look for words, and for ways of speaking, that rise out of and fall back into silence (or the other way round), words that lend themselves to the silence and are received back enriched. The silence can allow words to sink deep and do a new creative work in the dark.

Obviously, such words are not the vocabulary and manner of the railway station announcement. That is the everyday communication of necessary information, one directional, not expecting a response, and of relevance only to some of those who hear. Think rather of the words shared quietly by a small group, or courteously even in the vast spaces of a cathedral, the latter a new phenomenon when a sophisticated sound system is in place. The silence is more profound when voices reach you quietly from nearby rather than hurled at you from some distant high place. It may be true that in our day we are approaching wonder through intimacy rather than at a distance (where it is often entangled with display and grandeur, ambivalent bedfellows of fear and coercive power).

Prayers on the radio have had to learn this lesson. You have to take risks with pauses if the words are not to feel intrusive. After all, the loudspeaker is simply one other person in the kitchen or bedroom. Silence and words in such circumstances can penetrate each other, carrying the participant deeper than we may often realise.

This strong yet gentle connection of words and silence is not easy to achieve. So many of the words we use in public prayer have worn smooth over the centuries. They have lost their bite and their power to connect. So we wander off in our own silences, which are then too often filled with thoughts of no consequence. Then there are the words that batter us, that reduce us to the silence of fear. Also the words of rhetoric and oratory: they provoke feelings and action, but the response is often merely a reaction – quick and superficial. It is all very well to be on the move with slogans and alleluias, but I have a deep suspicion of political and religious rallies that cheapen both words and silence, and again reduce us to the less than fully human. By contrast, courteous words of invitation do not provoke an immediate reaction. Parables do not thrust truth at you. You are left to reflect, to pause, to be silent, to ruminate, and only then to respond, a response that is informed by the silence and reflection. The silence can hold, contain, and transform all that we bring to it, and allow wonder, attentiveness, and love to surface, a new awareness of who we are and what we can do, a quiet determination to act, and to do so with courage, and in our turn, with courtesy.

At the Sunday Eucharist in Grace Cathedral in San Francisco, with a large congregation in a splendid building, the 'servant of communion' (I refuse to say 'president') focused our minds and hearts on our own connectedness with the bread and wine which he held before us, with these words, with pauses after each phrase: 'Receive who you are . . . Become what you see . . .' The subsequent silence was full to overflowing.

The last words of this article are not mine. I read them at breakfast this morning in *The Tablet* (24 January 1998). Michael Paul Gallagher of the Gregorian University in Rome writes of God as Trinity and refers to an Italian theologian Bruno Forte, who has written a book the title of which translates as 'Trinity for Atheists', and in which he 'explores the interplay between Silence and Word in how we experience a tripersonal God. There is the Silence of the Father as origin, the eloquent Word of the Son as saviour, and the intimate silence of the Spirit, guiding us towards our end in love.'

I'm a fool: the JM Annual Retreat 2001

GRAHAM JOHNSON

> *When you enter into a relationship with God there are times when you feel very much at home with God and times when you are left feeling very foolish indeed . . .*

The most important part of the JM annual retreat is the retreat. It is not the gathering together of people from JM, though it is a great help and joy to be with others who are sympathetic to the fostering of contemplative prayer. It is not the mellifluous words of the conductor, though these can sometimes aid us in our devotion. It is not the beautiful surroundings of Launde Abbey, though its grounds and chapel can add to our spiritual awareness. It is the retreat that matters. It is the opportunity to let God be God for you. It is the chance to take a real break, to play truant. To stop doing all the things that we think are important. God is saying: 'Don't you dare line me up with all those weighty matters of everyday life that require your urgent attention. You can stop doing all those important things you do in your capacity as god and allow me to be God for the weekend. Enter into the silence but do not use it for your own ends. I am not just asking you to be still, but to be still and know that I am God.'

Although I have conducted many retreats yet I have to say that I am usually very nervous at the start of a retreat because I am never sure of the role of the conductor. We talk of silence and then bring along a man or woman who talks to us. The silence becomes full of words that are often distractions. T.S. Eliot sums up for me what the words of the conductor should be – they are

> only hints and guesses
> Hints followed by guesses; and the rest
> Is prayer, observance, discipline, thought and action
> The hint half guessed, the gift half understood is Incarnation.
> (Stanza 5 of 'The Dry Salvages')

Nevertheless, the 'hints and guesses' that I shall be giving will relate to the circumstances of playing truant with God in retreat, for we find ourselves in an unusual situation (perhaps not so unusual for those who practise contemplative prayer) that the 'prayer, observance, discipline, thought and action' give us a heightened awareness of the seeming presence of God or the seeming absence of God. Scripture may tell us that it is a dangerous thing to fall into the hands of the living God. Experience teaches us that when you enter into a relationship with God there are times when you feel very much at home with God and times when you are left feeling very foolish indeed, wondering just where you are and where God is in this relationship.

It is these feelings I want to explore in the talks during the retreat. Its title 'I'm a fool – you're a fool' comes from a reflection on the life and work of Anthony de Mello. In the last two years I have been giving retreats under the title 'Contemplation and Awareness in the Writings of Julian of Norwich and Anthony de Mello'. Those who know me will expect me to enjoy de Mello's sometimes humorous stories but what I most like about him is his openness to change. Others may find this a difficulty and want some authoritative teaching, but if our relationship with God is to grow then we must change because change is part of growth. In his early teaching, de Mello laid stress on accepting yourself as you are, a human being loved by God. The people at his retreats had to be able to say, 'I'm OK, you're OK.' Yet before his death, de Mello was teaching people, 'I'm a fool, you're a fool.' In fact both are right but at different times. A person recently converted to Christianity has a wonderful feeling of 'I am OK. I am loved, accepted, forgiven, saved by God.' But as the relationship develops there come times when faced with what you now feel about God you know that you are a gibbering idiot! It is this sense of foolishness that I want to explore in the time of retreat. First, in order to reassure people who feel the same way, and second to try to show that it appears to be necessary in our relationship with God.

As a spiritual director I come across people who experience this in their life whether it be church, marriage, family, work, or socially related – all are part of our prayer relationship. It may be experienced as a direct absence of God, or a loss of passion for some job or some person that previously was of great importance to us. It may be in a call to do something that seems beyond the call of duty or your ability or what your friends would expect of you. Not only does God seem absent but so does every support around you.

If this is not your experience, don't be put off coming to the retreat. I repeat that it is the retreat that matters.

Reflections on a JM retreat at Launde Abbey

JENNY SMEED

God's presence is very tangible in this place.

Approaching the Elizabethan manor house down a long winding driveway, a wonderful patchwork of fields unfolds intersected with trees and walls, some dotted with sheep and cows, some freshly ploughed, drawing the eye ever upward to the horizon.

The imposing mellow brickwork of the house exudes an aura of calm in the late afternoon light, radiating a tranquillity of spirit gained over hundreds of years and passed on to present-day pilgrims.

The twelfth-century chapel is the only original part of the Priory to be found. It lies at the rear of the house surrounded by a picturesque sunken garden. Almost full-length stained glass windows let in prisms of light, adding to the peace of centuries of devotion.

The stables, transformed into accommodation, lie opposite a pond where water lilies and various species of duck vie for space. Martins and wagtails skim the surface then climb away into the sky after the insects brought out by the warm autumn temperatures.

The view from the rear stable windows shows fields with young trees and on one side a children's play area. A yellow rose blooms directly beneath the window, along with golden rod and its attendant bees and hover-flies.

Walking towards the house in the late evening dusk, peace immeasurable, healing solace, a welling up of emotions from deep solitude, tears overflowing, joy and sadness intermingled for past losses, present times and future hopes. How much can be conveyed without words. A look, smile, lifted eyebrow, gesture, touch of the hand, blown kiss. The true love of God does not always need the spoken word.

Grey clouds overcast the sky, the wind holding its breath, air completely still, a distant field illumined briefly as the sun peeps through, only to disappear in the blink of an eye. God's presence is very tangible in this place. With no words to crowd out his 'still small voice', thoughts wander at will giving him time and space to reach out and touch our minds.

Five o'clock in the morning. The mist lying thick across the fields, cooling the atmosphere, not yet quite light, owls still calling out to each other, two ducks decide to have a sudden squabble, then all is peaceful again. A walk around the grounds listening to sheep munching the grass as rabbits scuttle into the undergrowth, their white tails bobbing. The leaves on the trees look very autumnal now, rustling slightly as the faintest breeze brushes them with its fingertips.

Time to leave, too soon, too soon, newly made friends departing for all parts of the country, one to South Africa. Hopefully some of the 'peace of the Lord' will stay and uphold in home and workplace. God bless.

The following five pieces came out of the retreat held in September 1994, marking JMs' twenty-first anniversary.

High Leigh without words

MICHAEL TILEY

A memorable weekend of sights, sounds, smells and silences.

Our retreat was reported in *The Tablet* (24 September 1994) as follows:

> WITHOUT WORDS
> Last weekend 178 people met at High Leigh Conference Centre to spend a weekend together in silence. They were celebrating the 21st birthday of their network of local groups, the Julian Meetings, which support with silent weekly meetings those who make a daily practice of silent contemplative prayer. There are 280 Julian Meetings around the United Kingdom, with further groups in Australia, South Africa and the United States.
>
> The Julian Meetings take Julian of Norwich as their patron, and they welcome all those who pray in silence, no matter what their church background or what their "method" for entering the silence.
>
> Because the gathering was ecumenical, the Sunday worship consisted – as is usual in their annual retreats – of a ceremony like the Eucharist but with an empty paten and an empty chalice. Like Teilhard de Chardin in his 'Mass on the World', they were consecrating their lives and their world, in circumstances where Communion was not possible.
>
> The well-known Anglican priest-doctor, Martin Israel, led the weekend, and the participants remained in the room for half an hour in silent prayer after listening to each address, as well as spending the weekend in a 'great silence' up until the Sunday worship, which was followed by a noisy party.

The 'noisy party', complete with an amazing birthday cake baked and decorated by Sue Brock, speeches and sparkling white wine, made a memorable weekend of sights, sounds, smells and silences. These impressions were skilfully woven together and reflected in Martin Israel's four addresses on prayer and the teachings of Mother Julian. Here are some personal impressions, which can only attempt to provide some verbal snapshots of the weekend.

Sights: Gentle smiles of recognition and friendship in the silence . . . Martin Israel's smile as he spoke . . . candles, plants, seasonal rich brown horse chestnuts, stones, sand, and other focuses for meditation in a dozen or so sub-group rooms . . . the *JM Magazine* editor, Pam Fawcett, providing a welcome massage on the floor to a retreatant with a back problem . . . High Leigh's quirky late Victorian architecture with unexpected corners, stairs, vistas, and gracious grounds of grass and woods.

Sounds: Country birds in nearby woods . . . the soft rumble of one hundred and seventy-eight pairs of soft soles heading purposefully and gently as a body to and from rooms, dining hall, lecture hall . . . the incurable sharp click of my bedroom door catch which would have passed unnoticed in daily life . . . the hushed rustle of paper turned by fingers exploring bookstall books (including newly published copies of *Circles of Silence*) . . . the tinkle of coins and rustle of bank notes quietly deposited . . . the soft clatter of plates and cutlery during meals . . . the occasional whispered requests for water, or salt . . . the quiet crockle of tea and coffee cups on saucers.

Smells: All pleasant, including the approach of welcome meals . . . a nearby farm . . . plants newly washed by a light shower . . . snuffed candles as an afterglow to our group meditations.

Silences: Variations in depth and length . . . following the addresses . . . in sub-groups during daylight and in candlelit darkness . . . the Mass on the World with its deep emptiness . . . gaps and cracks . . . goings in and comings out 'like a bucket in a well' (Chaucer's *Knight's Tale*) . . . sick and suffering friends and situations somehow blessed by our intercessions and silences . . . inwards and outwards in a gentle rhythm of peace and love.

During 'The preparation of the gifts' at Sunday worship

JUNE PLAICE

You came, Lord:
Unexpected, You came;
The honoured Guest,
Presence, known by Absence.

You took me by surprise –
I thought it would be no big thing,
No special thing, Your absence,
Till tears welled in my eyes . . .

And then I knew.
The empty plate Your grieving heart,
The empty cup holds tears of pain . . .
So must it be, until in You
We are made whole again.

Julian Meetings and me

HILARY BURN

Contemplative prayer is not a quiet backwater in Christian life – it is a way of being challenged and changed.

Silent am I now and still, dare not in Thy presence move,
To my waiting soul reveal the secret of Thy love.
(Charles Wesley)

We live in a world of noise and bustle, even our churches can be so full of activity that there is nowhere to be quiet and calm. Morning services, very often, are joyous, outgoing, noisy times, with the whole Church family joining together, but with very little time for quiet prayer. The need to take oneself apart for peace and quiet prayer is now recognised. Prayer meetings, Quiet Days and retreats are no longer seen as unusual . . . they are part of Christian experience and are found to be the answer to the need for enlarging our experience of God in silent prayer. Right in the forefront of this change in emphasis in prayer is Julian Meetings. The coming of Julian Meetings has enabled members of all Churches to pray together across denominational boundaries – to form friendships and to strengthen their own, and each other's, prayer lives.

It is amazing to think that Julian Meetings is twenty-one years old!

And yet, it is hard to think back to a time when I was not connected with it. Perhaps I am not alone, and we all feel this as we celebrate this anniversary.

I came into Julian Meetings in 1974, and soon was asked to take over the task of posting the magazines, three times a year. There were then 250 subscribers, and it seemed a fairly easy task to undertake. In fourteen years I saw the numbers grow, not only of subscribers to over 1,200, but the Julian Meetings grew in influence and seemed to be everywhere. When I first joined, there were no other silent prayer groups. The peace and strength of silent prayer together was an unknown quantity to many Christians. And yet the need was there. There were many people just waiting for a chance to find their place in such groups, as the rapid growth of Julian Meetings has shown. Suddenly their needs were recognised, and silence was valued. Countless letters reached me, expressing the gratitude of active church members, who had felt the lack of contemplative prayer in their Christian experience, and here it was! Following this recognition many churches now have their own prayer meetings, and are finding new strength in their members and in their fellowships. This influence has come from Julian Meetings, and can be felt in all denominations.

It has been a great privilege to have been part of the growth of Julian Meetings, and to have had a contribution to make. It has brought a great change in my own life. Contemplative prayer is not a quiet backwater in Christian life – it is a way of being challenged and changed. One has to have the courage to go forward and to answer God's call.

Through Julian Meetings I have made friends whose own experience has been similar to mine, and friends whose church background has been totally different from mine. We have been led forward in our Christian service and we all acknowledge the debt of gratitude to Julian Meetings as the starting point to the changes we have experienced.

Julian Meetings has given a new openness to my Christian faith, has shown me a fresh and exciting way to pray, to serve, and to answer the challenge to go forward in Christ. This I am sure is the experience of many others for whom contemplative prayer has become an essential part of life.

May we continue to go forward together.

A very happy birthday Julian Meetings – go from strength to strength!

Further distractions

On the tenth anniversary of JM Graham Johnson allowed his distractions in prayer to get the better of him. Sadly, eleven years later he has had another distraction.

As I stood in the checkout queue at the supermarket, my face gazed back at me from the *Living* magazine on the rack. My wife was away. I was buying for myself. With no one to talk to I thought back to the moment that had led to all this.

It was the report of the twenty-first anniversary Julian Meeting retreat that had started it all. Not just the participants but the national press had been amazed that nearly two hundred people had kept silent for more than twenty-four hours. It was featured in the *Guinness Book of Records* and this led to other groups trying to beat the record. The Methodist Retreat Association had two hundred and fifty people in silence for eight days. Not to be outdone, a Jesuit Cardinal called together five hundred of his crack Nineteenth Annotation Division for thirty days of silence. The Pentecostals would have been the first to have one thousand people for fifty days but for a fire in the roof above their heads. Retreat houses could no longer cope with the floods of people attempting the individual record, the record time for silence for a church council, the choir silence record. There were rumours of drug-taking and incense sniffing. Bishops had to adjudicate as to whether it was permissible to arrange flowers during the silence. It was when Christians started turning their conservatories into hermitages or their potting-sheds into poustinias that the inspiration took over the whole nation. The desire for silence, otherwise known as the JM Blessing, began to sweep the land. The House of Commons, fearing a silent Prime Minister's Question Time, tried to halt the Blessing, but the nation knew what it wanted. Parliament was dissolved and in a new election, Doctor Martin Israel's party, the Silent Majority, swept into power with the promise of a Retreat House in every street.

The regular daily stoppages for silence across the nation really began when a radical theatre manager adopted a five-minute silence before every performance in place of the national anthem. Then it was noticed football crowds were deserting pubs in order to be in their places for the fifteen-minute silence before the game. The old monastic pattern of Prime, Terce, Sext, None and Vespers was adopted with traffic, factories and schools coming to a standstill for five minutes at 6 a.m., 9 a.m., 12 noon, 3 p.m., and 6 p.m. People no longer boasted how quickly they had made their journey. They delighted in roadworks and hold-ups that caused them to stop and have time to contemplate on their journey. At Waterloo Station crash barriers were erected to control the crowds of business people wanting to catch the channel tunnel train that always broke down – thus giving ample time for leisurely silence on their expense accounts.

As people listened to God, they began to listen to one another. They listened to the poor, the deprived, the inadequate, and all who cried out for justice. The Silent Majority party had no trouble in raising taxes to pay for housing, health and long-awaited social reforms. Ten per cent of GNP was given to Overseas Development but it was not needed, for by then the JM Blessing had swept the world.

Christian Unity had happened several years ago. As Christians came closer to God in the silence, so they came so close to one another that denominational labels ceased to exist. Nevertheless a current issue still taxing the Synods was the women's debate. Women were demanding shorter working hours than men to allow them more time to carry out St Paul's command that women should keep silent (1 Timothy 2:12).

'Ooh! Mr Johnson,' said the young man at the checkout, 'I am sorry they didn't make you Archbishop of York. I voted for you. But I think that nice Mrs Wakeman will make a good job of it. Wonderful news about your wife though, I read it in that magazine. What does it feel like to be husband of the Pope?'

The JM Twenty-first Retreat had a lot to answer for!

Not being Charlotte

HILARY WAKEMAN

> *I believe that coming together to pray in silence is the best, the deepest and the most natural way we experience ecumenicity.*

Anniversaries invite the reviewing of how things are. Given the anniversary of a birth, a marriage or a death, or the ending of a year or decade or century and the beginning of another, our instinct is to take a step-back view; to assess the past and look to the future.

With the twenty-first anniversary last year of the founding of the Julian Meetings we have done quite a lot of looking at the past. I would like now to look to the future and where we think the movement might be going. But this is a personal view. What follows is my own thinking and should not be taken as any indication of the way the movement as a whole might be moving. We are as non-hierarchical as it is possible to be without falling into chaos, and my function, as the accidental founder and apparently long-term Convener of the Julian Meetings, is inevitably ambivalent: but it is neither that of a spiritual nor an administrative dictator.

All the same, JM and what it does is very precious to me, and I live (as I suspect many do, not least the members of the Advisory Group) with an undergirding sense of what it is about and how it is developing. This sense, for me, consists of an interweaving of gratitude, thanksgiving and assessment. Rather like a pesky small child in a rowboat, I feel I must keep an eye on the speed, the direction and the list even though I am not strong enough to row.

Where I hope we are going now is onwards. At the time of our tenth anniversary I wrote in the Magazine that I hoped that before we reached our twentieth the prayer of silence would become such a normal part of church life that JM could cease to exist. That hasn't happened. Perhaps the very hope that it could was skewed. In the first place because no matter how much silence becomes part of organised worship, contemplative prayer is for most of us something that needs to happen at times and places other than during services of word and/or sacrament. And secondly because coming together to pray in silence, the way we do in JM, is such a short cut to ecumenical unity. I believe that for thousands of us, it is the best, the deepest and the most natural way we experience ecumenicity.

If there is any change of direction I would like to see in the near future it would be towards a gentle increase in promoting the practice of meditation or contemplative prayer. One of the reasons we need to be in existence still is that there are still millions who could be blessed by it but do not know it. If we who have received that gift don't offer it to others, who will? We cannot leave it to the 'professionals' – clergy and ministers – because it is still sadly the case that many of them have no experience of it.

One of the joys of JM is that we are not high-powered. Yet I wonder if we are not confusing our laudable desire for minimal organisation with an aversion to whatever publicity is necessary to ensure that the greatest possible number of people know what meditation really is. Are we also confusing our desire to be non-directive in the matter of suggesting how people might pray with whatever direction-indicators are necessary if people are not to become lost? I wonder if we are not being altogether too polite, too genteel. I am reminded of the anonymous rhyme:

> Charlotte, having seen his body
> Borne before her on a shutter,
> Like a well-conducted person
> Went on cutting bread and butter.

It is not entirely apposite: in our experience of contemplative prayer we do not generally see horror, more likely the lower edges of heaven; all the same, we carry on as if nothing had changed. I'm not suggesting we should engage in billboard advertising, that we should go out into the highways and hedges and compel people to come in, that we should become public nuisances on the subject of meditation. But I am suggesting we go more in that direction than we have done; that we should stop being Charlottes. Specifically, we could more actively promote JM through existing ecumenical structures. We could offer local speakers on the subject of Christian meditation to the sorts of meetings or groups that are always looking out for speakers. We could be more thorough about getting supplies of our leaflets into churches, retreat houses, libraries, clubs. We could encourage friends and acquaintances in other countries to start groups. Great numbers of people are vaguely interested in meditation but don't know how to start: on a regional basis we could offer free tuition sessions, advertising them in local papers.

Many of us find ourselves with JM precisely because we haven't wanted the seemingly limiting methods, techniques or mantras that other meditation groups offer. And so we tend to veer away from any suggestion of being directive: for example of pressing the desirability of the daily practice of this way of prayer. Yet I wonder if we don't do ourselves and each other a disservice in this? Quite often someone in a group will enthuse about the monthly or fortnightly meeting in such a way that it is clear he or she is not meditating on the days in between. How sad. None of us wants to be the one to say, 'Oh but you should, you don't know what you're missing' – and yet it's what the rest are probably thinking. It would be good to be more open about that.

I would hope we can continue to question and, if and when necessary, change old ways of doing things. For example, this year our annual retreat will be led not by an individual conductor but a group of people, each of them drawing around them a circle of retreatants, and at times coming together as the full group. This follows from our experience of small groups in the retreat last year. They were needed because the retreat was unusually large: but what came out of necessity was found to be a blessing, and so we hope to explore the benefits further this year.

I also hope we can do more in the future in the way of awareness of the interaction of body and soul (not expecting to meditate straight after a meal!) and the influence of the visual or aesthetic dimension in our preparations for prayer (some react more to this than others).

Last and largest of all, I hope that by our own faithful practice of this praying we can play a part in the urgent need to draw together what are too often seen as opposites: 'religion' and 'the world'. In contemplative prayer we learn to be at home with God; and if we are at home with God there is no place and no time where we are not at home. If we are at one with God there is no person with whom we are not at one, no people of whom we are not part. What better hope is there for the Kingdom in this world and the next than that all people should know this unity within themselves?

SECTION NINE

'Crafting the pattern': out into the wider world

A poem from Tasmania – on the death of a tree

DOREEN THURSTON

I have watched you slowly dying
    and I grieve for you,
for what you once were when I first saw you.

Then you were full of life in your maturity;
    spreading green shade and welcome walnuts in season,
    eagerly sought after by locals who came
    with their bags and buckets.
Your life was guarded and unthreatened . . .

Then came the developers –
to build and benefit by a restaurant,
    necessitating the provision of a
    large car park.

But you, gracious tree, local landmark,
were not to be removed.
    You had an order on you to be saved –
    the concrete to be restricted by a
    small margin of earth around your sturdy body.
So we rejoiced that you would remain supreme
    over man's puny insensitivity.

I have watched you struggle,
    and suffer, to recover from the throb of
    man's machinery,
    violating your foundations,
    cutting off the source of life-giving
    moisture from your spreading roots.

I have seen you, by day and night,
    surrounded by vehicles, vibrating

and belching out poisonous fumes
into your pure atmosphere.
You could not win.

Now I see your almost naked branches,
here, in the midst of summer,
when you should be fully clothed
and bearing precious fruit
And I cry for you
because you are dying –
majestic, life giving, glorious tree.
Forgive me . . . 'the whole creation groans . . . '

Celtic knot

ANN LEWIN

The tangled roots from which I spring
nourish my depths and
send out shoots for growth;
separate yet entwined
friends, relatives, strangers
and people I don't like.
We grow together in
intricate relationship.

Weaver God, pick up
the threads of my experience,
craft the pattern, and
in your time
reveal significance.

Spirituality and church worship - mind the gap!

ANGELA ASHWIN

Church services need spaces in which to let the words breathe.

'My spiritual life has blossomed in retreats, meditation groups and guided prayer, but I struggle with church worship.' I often hear comments like this. They come from lay people, and also from clergy who long to enable their congregations to discover the richness of silence and to help them engage more prayerfully with the liturgy. There are also thousands of church-goers who never go on retreat or join a prayer group and are cautious about such things. So the gap between spirituality and worship is there too.

Of course many people feel spiritually nourished by church worship, which, in turn, flows into their everyday prayer. But many of us do not. I believe that we need to explore ways in which spirituality and corporate worship can enrich each other, rather than ending up as two separate and unconnected worlds.

We can easily feel that the world of silent prayer and spiritual exercises is where things really happen between us and God, and that 'church on Sunday' is just a tedious extra. Yet it doesn't have to be like this, and our faith could become too individualistic if we had no sense of belonging to the whole Body of Christ. On the other hand, it is vital that people who lead and plan services listen to those who talk about the contemplative dimension in worship. On a practical level, church services need spaces in which to let the words breathe. Sermons and prayers can be used imaginatively, to encourage meditative prayer. A well-prepared introduction to worship can quieten a congregation, as can reflective music, sensitive use of physical space and a visual focus.

There are many ways in which everyday prayer can make a difference to our church worship. Put bluntly, we worship better if we pray in the rest of our lives as well. For example, if we regularly spend time quietly with God, that should help us to 'pray the words' in church more attentively, and to worship with a less cluttered mind. This is not about achieving anything, but about being more open to God. When we are listening with heart as well as head, even a line from a well-worn hymn may suddenly leap out and touch us. It's worth asking ourselves whether we arrive in church with much expectation or trust that God will speak to us.

Furthermore, the silence of adoration reminds us that prayer and worship are for God's sake, before our own. It's easy to slip into a market-place mentality, and become so anxious to get something out of church services that we forget that we are there first of all to give. As in all of the spiritual life, a great deal hangs on our intention and desire, simply to be there for God, and to bring the world's needs before him. The Spirit is present and active, redeeming and making good our worship, even when we don't feel very much ourselves (though that's no excuse for badly-led or ill-prepared worship!).

Finally, worship can spill over into the rest of life and get into our bloodstream. We can take a phrase from a church service, and weave it into everyday life, breathing it in as we walk, singing it in the bath, digging it into the garden, painting it during a prayer-time, and, in the end, sitting still with it. Thus we build up a memory-bank that links us not only with our own congregation but also with the world-wide Church of past and present, and the communion of saints in heaven. Whether we are praying alone or worshipping in church, our offering is swept up into the ceaseless praise of the saints and angels. What an encouragement!

Doxological

JOY FRENCH

I don't want Halleluyahs,
    Growled the Father;
Nor all those Praises,
    Added the Son;
Nor Ave Marias,
    Murmured the Mother,
    Packing up nappies
    For some Holy Innocents
    (Jewish or Muslim?
    She wasn't worried.)

The Spirit sighed:
Gloria in Excelsis?
I'd rather see the glory
Of a good deed
In this naughty world.
O humanity, humanity,
When will you get it right?

The bishop and negative space

JOHN HAWKINS

After the Reformation the Word became the pre-eminent symbol within western culture. This is now changing.

In art and architecture, 'negative space' is significant. Painters often concentrate on the interesting shapes formed by the spaces between the objects being painted. For architects like myself 'spaces between' can be as important as the actual buildings. It is always instructive to listen to the 'empty spaces' – what is left out or brushed aside – in the speeches of politicians. And, it seems, of bishops.

On the first Sunday in June, a group of Ministers In Secular Employment gathered to hear a lecture by their Bishop on 'Changes in Church and Society'.

The Bishop found it 'interesting' that despite the decline in institutional religion, there had been a marked rise in the quest for spirituality. His interest did not however extend beyond one dismissive sentence: 'Sometimes this is seen in fringe religion: paganism, satanism, New Age, new religious movements, astrology, and so on'. It is a very great pity that he had no time to expand on this subject. Using his own headings, I would like to suggest that the 'fringe' encompasses at least three important, even exciting, pointers to an emergent spirituality.

Firstly, a comprehensive theology of creation would speak of human beings as co-creator with God and of the arts as a window to the supreme Creator. It was only after the Reformation that the Word became the pre-eminent symbol within western culture. This is now changing, with non-verbal symbols becoming the common currency of computer users worldwide. At the same time, there is an interest and involvement in the arts unprecedented in history. Through the media, and direct access, millions are now familiar with great painting and artefacts (witness the popularity of, for example, The National Trust) while every home can enjoy good music (think of the phenomenal success of Classic FM). Meanwhile parish clergy (with honourable exceptions) continue to advocate the destruction of 'outworn plant' and to feed their flocks on aesthetic tat and musical pap.

Secondly, a theology of redemption needs surely to acknowledge that our salvation was wrought by means of Christ's bodily sacrifice, that Jesus' earthly ministry embraced much bodily healing and that, *ipso facto*, the body is important (despite the customary coyness of Christians towards it). The world of conventional medicine is now at last becoming aware of the inter-relationship of body, mind and spirit. This was a matter of common knowledge in earlier times and has long been known to practitioners of the complementary therapies, which the Church continues to regard with enormous suspicion.

Thirdly, what the Bishop calls a theology of the Spirit needs to recognise the continuing growth of the contemplative prayer and retreat movements, often attracting not only card-carrying church members but also the increasing fellowship of the disenchanted, and even (heaven help us!) rank outsiders. Such enterprises as the Holy Island Project involve members of all the world's major faiths: an engagement not congenial to the majority of Christians who still regard people like Moslems as quite outside the pale. But it is hard to imagine a more powerful symbol of reconciliation in our divided world.

What gives me the impression that the Church 'just doesn't want to know'?

Contemplative prayer and the future of Christianity

HILARY WAKEMAN

In meeting together to share and support the practice of contemplative prayer we are on a path of hope for Christianity.

To say that 'the world has changed' after the attacks on the USA on 11 September 2001 has become a cliché; but one that affects our daily lives and our future.

Not perhaps from the same causes and not quite as suddenly, but with effects every bit as deep, religion too has changed, especially Christianity. Not perhaps since the sixteenth century has the Church faced such an unknown future. The influence of New Age thinking, the continuing impact of science, the growing distrust of authoritarianism, the writings of Bishops John Spong and Richard Holloway, of Bede Griffiths and Don Cupitt, and suddenly so many others like them: all of these show a Christianity that is shifting and slipping. Some people retreat to the security of fundamentalism. Most are being gradually moved, even while they think they are standing firm. Which is just as well: the alternative to our moving is surely the end of Christianity.

There is much evidence that many of the old ways of talking about God carry no meaning for people now, or are actually repulsive; that doctrinal statements which in early Christian times sought to put flesh on abstract ideas are heard as concrete statements in modern ears and are quietly denied in modern hearts. We are like a vast crowd looking at the parade of Christianity and thinking, if not actually saying, that the Emperor has no clothes on. Mostly we are not saying it because we are afraid of hurting the people around us, whom we imagine to be still believing in that marvellous suit of clothes. For a while we stay at the roadside, supported by the apparent belief of those around us. In the end we silently slip away, and go no more to the parades. And the crowd becomes smaller and smaller (apart from the areas where new people, looking in, are told about the marvellous suit of clothes, and so much want to be part of such enthusiasm that they do indeed see them). The crowd shrinks, but the parade of the unclothed Emperor goes on.

It has been claimed for a long time that the problem lies in the widening gap between what the theologians are saying and what the people in the pews are hearing. The fault is said to be the clergy's, and the forecast has been that the gap will go on widening until disaster hits. Yet we go on papering over the gap, trying not to think about how many will fall when the paper splits.

The Churches have become spiritual juggernauts, vast structures stuck in the mud by their own weight. When people talk about 'the decline of the Church' I suspect that what they are describing is mainly a corporate disenchantment with the structures – and then church-going and the resultant sense of community is abandoned too.

At first glance it seems obvious to say that the more superficial our faith, the more fact-based it is, the less easily it will survive this crowd-thinning that Christianity is undergoing. Yet even the thinnest faith holds on for many reasons, including the security of habit and, not least, the comfort that is obtained in times of distress or sorrow. It would be dreadful if that was lost. But it need not be lost. The choice is not between faith-with-comfort and honesty-with-no-comfort.

Christianity can survive – if we are brave. The voices telling us this are getting louder, and in the end maybe the crowd will turn and listen. What will not survive in this new century are authoritarian, hierarchical (and therefore denominational) structures, finance-driven structures, and creeds and doctrines that need re-interpreting line by line before they can be spoken with honesty. What will survive is our experience of God, our 'knowing' God. And one of the deepest ways we know God is through contemplative prayer.

In the practice of contemplative prayer we enter a sense of God that is beyond ideas and concepts: we 'know' God and are content to know nothing about God. All we can say of God is that God is. 'I am that I am'. At best we can say that we sense a personal relationship, or that we feel aware of being sustained by a great love. All else is *glimpses* of God in our lives (e.g., Jesus, holiness, miracles), or a recording of such glimpses (e.g., the Bible, doctrine, creeds) that human weakness tries to set in concrete.

Which is why I believe that in meeting together to share and support the practice of contemplative prayer we are on a path of hope for Christianity. There already we have the setting aside of doctrinal statements and denominational claims. While respecting our traditions we do not impose belief-tests, or use a lot of words, which are so often belief-traps. We manage without setting some people up on pillars of supposed spiritual superiority: instead we value what each one has to offer. We need no special buildings, that will become idols or mill-stones, but we make ordinary places into 'sacred spaces' by praying there. We simply allow God to be God to us, and in sharing that experience we build community and strengthen our capacity to love others. What as we get older we increasingly know to be true in our personal lives will be seen to be true in our religious lives also: 'What will survive of us is love' (Philip Larkin, 'The Arundel Tomb').

Having recently retired from full-time parish ministry I am well aware that a faith that is too formless could become so vague as to disappear entirely. Certainly contemplative prayer needs a basis of story, both of myth and of godly people of the past, if it is to be fed. But just as our bodies know what foods they need and we do not all eat the same meals, so our souls too will draw the sustenance they need from what is available. Fears that this will lead to spiritual anarchy can be offset by seeing that behind that fear is often another, that of loss of authority. Yet Jesus managed with no larger power structure than the Spirit of God.

And what is true of Christianity is true also of all the major world faiths. Already we know of some Buddhists and Christians meditating together. Where will it all end? In hope for the world perhaps, and what we used to call in the old-fashioned symbolic language 'the Kingdom of God'.

Meditation – in a comprehensive school

POLLY SMALLWOOD

> *As the years progressed prayer battled with pupil self-consciousness and peer pressure.*

A friend who had once worked with the missions in central Africa told me that in Kiswahili the word for 'give' and the word for 'receive' were the same. I wish I knew this word, and that others understood it, for I am at a loss when other people ask me what I do.

Christ the King Catholic Comprehensive, where my three sons were educated, has a Chaplaincy Team of which I am a member. I have seen the same children, in groups of six, for the past three years. With the guidance of the teaching staff I interpret the class topic in my own way and relate this to prayer. The first year was easy going, the children co-operated fully and gave and received much. As the years progressed prayer battled with pupil self-consciousness and peer pressure.

I find the 'Seven Circles of Prayer', the method that uses silence and scripture reading, extremely helpful, so I decided to adapt this to these thirteen-year-olds. We concentrated on a candle flame and breathed the name of Jesus. Our groups were a mixture of boys and girls. However, I did notice on occasions when girls were absent the boys were stilled and said they had enjoyed the meditation time. I decided to ask if, in their third year, we could have single gender groups. During the school holiday I read and explored Anthony de Mello's methods of prayer and decided to practise the Body Sensations method of meditation with a view to using it with the children.

I explain carefully to the children what we mean by Christian meditation: I make sure they understand that they cannot bring about a particular sensation. They lie on the carpeted floor for approximately seven minutes in silence. Then I read a phrase, poem, verse of hymn that fits in with the work we did before the meditation, again with Christ being the focus. I repeat this at intervals before telling them to sit up slowly. I ask if anyone wishes to say a prayer aloud. Prayers focus on silence or on God's all-embracing grace and love.

When the children want to stop

JULIE MCGUINNESS

Fact-based cognitive teaching can miss the essence of religious faith. Reflection Time is a welcome corrective to this.

Six-year-olds sit in a circle round a low, cloth-covered box that bears a lighted candle. Their lowered heads, crossed legs with hands resting on knees indicate they are in 'listening position' as gentle music plays. The activity is Reflection Time. It was developed by Linda White, a deputy head teacher with Nottingham LEA's Task Force, whose book *Reflection Time: Developing a Reflective Approach to Teaching and Learning* (Church House Pub., 2000) was the fruit of research undertaken when she was awarded the National Society's first Research Fellowship in 1998. Mrs White's approach to teaching stresses the quality of classroom relationships. Reflection Time is at its heart. She thinks it has a beneficial effect on children's behaviour, and helps create an effective learning environment. It also has a spiritual resonance, although she did not initially develop it with this in mind.

It started with Circle Time, an established element in primary education where children sit together as the school day ends, talking in turn about something important to them. Mrs White introduced the act of lighting a candle as a calming focus, and then worked on the children's body language, discovering how a special sense of attentiveness was engendered when the class all adopted a particular posture. She introduced the activity at different times in the day, perhaps to calm children after the excitement of a windy playtime; or to provide a structured way of refocusing their attention between learning activities.

'The ever-increasing curriculum requirements mean the school day can feel demanding. Sometimes they need a moment to take stock.' Gradually Reflection Time emerged as a quiet ritual to offset the hectic school day. It now follows an established routine. Individual children have particular jobs to do in the setting-up of central candle, cloth and water-jug. Once the children are in position round the lighted candle, a short piece of meditative music is played. They can request the day's music from a selection that includes Pachelbel's *Canon* and Native American chants. After that they pass round a stone. The stone-holder can pass it on in silence or speak out thoughts. These can range from sadness at the death of a pet to delight at the prospect of fish and chips for tea. Its time-slot varies. 'The children often ask for it. I try to respond to the classroom dynamics. Spirituality is not compartmentalised. It is there as we discuss the feelings music can evoke, or in science lessons in children's wonder as they learn how to make a shadow. Young children delight in those natural, magical things that adults often miss.'

The one scheduled slot is just before Religious Education. Mrs White says the children's reverent approach spills over into RE: 'If I produce religious artefacts, the children instinctively handle them with care. They have somehow picked up a sense of their sacredness. I don't know how I could convey this in any other way.' What about Reflection Time's relationship to RE? Trevor Cooling, head of the Stapleford Centre, an independent Christian education centre, thinks that fact-based cognitive teaching can miss the essence of religious faith, and he sees Reflection Time as a welcome corrective to this. Drawing parallels between children's own experience and what goes on in religions can build a bridge of understanding, he says. But it does raise questions. Such emphasis on the experiential approach implies that at root religion is about human experience, of which all religions are equally valid expressions. 'It ignores the vital issue of the truth claims inherent in different religious beliefs. We need to exercise spiritual discernment. Do we see children's experience as instrumental in understanding religion, or as an end in itself?'

Skills of discernment may well emerge among Mrs White's pupils, as her focus in Reflection Time at present is on encouraging children to value the chance to think. 'We need to give them time to develop their thinking by questioning things and working them through. It's something that's easily lost in a busy day.'

The Prison Phoenix Trust

SANDRA CHUBB

> *Practising meditation, for the first time ever I begin to see a tiny spark in myself which I like.*

We're All Doing Time. That is the title of a book which The Prison Phoenix Trust sends out free on request to prisoners all over the UK as part of its work which recognises that even prisoners can find freedom – through meditation.

The Trust recognises that many people choose to go on retreat, to places just like prison, where small bare rooms, isolated from friends and families, give them a chance to find out just who they really are.

'In dealing with the problems of drugs, violence and offending behaviour, we are confronted with the inner presence of a kind of foreign element,' says Director Sister Elaine MacInnes. 'Undoubtedly, such palliatives as medicines and therapy are helpful, and we heartily endorse their use. We know also that the treatment for addiction employed by Alcoholics Anonymous has one of the highest reputations in the world today. Its basic assumption is that addicts must believe in some power greater than themselves.'

The Trust's way not only underlines this basis, but also teaches that this power is available at all times and is very close at hand, for it is within us all. The oriental disciplines that The Prison Phoenix Trust recommends that the teachers associated with it should use, not only have those same presuppositions, but are also designed to use that very power, for healing. For convenience sake, they use yoga to address the body and meditation for the mind, but as a matter of fact, both overlap. These holistic disciplines allow the power that dwells within to work in its most natural way, and invariably when this happens, prisoners say they feel refreshed.

'The key word is "allow" . . . the procedure is to allow the healing to happen, and not make it happen, which is a most welcome change in itself,' adds Sister Elaine. 'The oriental masters say that offensive behaviour is caused by an over-active ego, which becomes the chief operating agent, and acts only for itself. How refreshing to be free of this inner pressure.'

There is much documented experience in the healing of violence and offending behaviour as a result of yoga and meditation.

Addiction, whether a disease or learned, is a separate problem, but there is sufficient evidence that living with addiction is not a lost cause.

'Allowing the inner power to heal body and mind is surely a gain of inestimable measure to all practitioners. We see this inner power as the source of the Sacred. Considering the present-day climate towards religion, we do not feel it necessary to stress this point. Nor is there any debate as to the tags and names available,' continues Sister Elaine.

Prisons are full of Christians, Moslems, Buddhists, Rastas, Hindus, Jews and many other people following religious faiths. They are also full of people who have no faith at all. 'However,' Sister Elaine adds, 'it behoves us not to overlook the fact that we are in a training which allows the Sacred to work in its own appropriate way.' Since a large majority of prisoners have drug and drink addiction histories, the meditation which The Phoenix Trust espouses is a safe and simple one. Based on the premise of silent body, silent mind, prisoners are encouraged to sit erect and practise meditation on the breath, using an easy breath-counting technique.

As one young offender and former addict, who had been self-harming for several years, put it recently, 'There has never been a time when I have felt happy about myself. But since reading *We're All Doing Time* and practising meditation for six days, for the first time ever, I begin to see a tiny spark in myself which I like.'

The Prison Phoenix Trust finds and trains teachers who are mature in their own practice, to teach in prisons, and it supports them with regular workshops. The Trust corresponds with inmates who are confronted by an awareness of their own spirituality during imprisonment, and supports thousands of men and women who have discovered that daily practices like yoga and meditation can help them free themselves – and others – of an intolerable burden.

As well as *We're All Doing Time* by Bo Lozoff, two other books called *Lineage* and *Just Another Spiritual Book* by the same author (published by Humankindness Foundation, 1985, 1988 and 1990, respectively), are sent out free of charge to prisoners on request. People who begin to deepen their meditation practice and wish for a little further guidance, can then be supported by *Being Free Through Meditation* by Sister Elaine (Prison Phoenix Trust, 1995), which is a digest of her book called *Teaching Zen to Christians* (re-issued as *Light Sitting in Light*, Zen Centre for Oriental Spirituality in the

Philippines, 1999). Word of the Trust has been spread almost entirely by word of mouth amongst inmates. The initiative for making contact with the Trust comes from them too.

The Trust has the warm support of one of its patrons Judge Stephen Turnim, (the former) Chief Inspector of Prisons, and in 1994 the annual Prison Governors' Conference asked The Prison Phoenix Trust to run workshops on three days of the conference. Nevertheless, the Oxford-based charity runs on a financial shoestring, without government funding. 'It's difficult to raise support for positive work with prisoners in these days of rising crime,' admits Sister Elaine. 'But even when we are down to our last month's reserves, we don't despair. God's providence speaks through people.'

Note: Sister Elaine MacInnes, a Canadian Catholic nun, spent fifteen years in Japan as a missionary where she studied meditation. She was transferred to the Philippines in 1976 and was one of the first two Catholics to become an accredited Roshi (or Zen teacher). During her seventeen years in the Philippines, Sister Elaine taught meditation to political prisoners who had been badly tortured under the Marcos regime. Some years after his release, one prisoner, the famous politician Horatio 'Boy' Morales, when asked for the peak experience of his life, replied, 'The *kensho* experience I had in prison.'

Meditation - a New Age phenomenon?

ADRIAN B. SMITH

> *The development of a deeper consciousness . . . has brought Christians to the realisation that a lot of church life is lived at the surface.*

The expression 'New Age Movement' provokes a whole range of reactions among Christians. Or perhaps it would be more true to say it evokes different reactions across the whole range of the Christian Church. At one end of the spectrum are members of Pentecostal churches to whom the phrase is like a red rag to a bull. To them everything falling under that title is not only non-Christian (and for that reason not acceptable) but anti-Christian and even Satanic.

Numerous are the booklets and tracts published in recent years to prove as much.

At the other end of the spectrum are some widely known and widely respected theological voices who, if not taking the New Age label to themselves, are certainly encouraging us to have a new vision of life and its spiritual dimension in terms which any 'new-ager' would recognise. I am thinking of Teilhard de Chardin, Bede Griffiths, Kadichi Kadowaki, Matthew Fox. And now I notice that these are all at the Roman Catholic end of the spectrum, although not representative of Catholic theology as a whole. So perhaps the rag is not so red to a Papal Bull!

However, bulls or no bulls, the field of the 'New Age' is not clear and smooth but full of quagmires and mists and shady areas. I suggest that the label 'New Age Movement' is a label given by the media to an enormous range of phenomena that are increasingly becoming part of our western culture. In the 1960s it was the world of freaks and fringe people, in the 1970s it moved from the periphery towards the centre with our daughters becoming vegetarians and auntie going to yoga classes. In the 1980s New Age shops and book-stalls were more widely seen and most large towns opened their holistic health centres. Now in the 1990s it is decidedly part of our culture. Whether we agree or disagree with all or some of the phenomena that is presented as New Age, we cannot close our eyes to it and pretend it is non-existent. Nor can we pretend that it is not having an increasing influence on western values.

This whole range of phenomena – and I have a New Age dictionary with over 400 entries and even there I find several omissions – I suggest can be classified under three main heads. In other words these phenomena are indicative of three major trends in our western society. Namely:

1. A new era of awareness.
2. A movement towards greater unity, at three levels:
   - at the personal level of body-mind-spirit harmony
   - inter-person unity (ranging from the increase of communities to the unions formed by nations)
   - cosmic unity: humanity becoming more one with our environment.
3. A reaching for the spiritual dimension in personal lives.

These are hypothetical categories and there is no clear distinction between them. However, the increasing number of people taking up meditation confirms the point I am making. It features in the first trend, it has the unifying effect of the second trend and it is a fast-spreading practice because of the third.

But is meditation, as some Christians would claim, one of those phenomena that should be listed under the umbrella title of New Age?

As a way of prayer we find deep meditation appearing a long way back in Christian tradition: the desert fathers, John Cassian, the Russian Church, and later in the writings of the great mystics and *The Cloud of Unknowing*. Although there is no specific mention of this type of prayer in the life of Jesus, he showed all the signs of being a person living out of that deep consciousness that we regard as the fruit of meditation.

But I believe there are three ways in which we can regard meditation as 'new', as a phenomenon of our era of New Consciousness.

In the first place, it would appear that it is the coming to the West of eastern gurus in the 1960s, bringing us not a form of prayer, but a mental exercise, a means to deeper consciousness, that has caused us Christians in the West to re-examine our own tradition and to bring the ancient practice to the fore again.

Secondly, the new awareness amongst people, the development of a deeper consciousness, has led to a search for the spiritual dimension that people feel is missing from our very commodity-possessing society. So many people are turning away from pursuing quantity to pursuing quality of life: from human having to human being. This has brought Christians to the realisation that a lot of church life is lived at the surface, in an outer dimension: beliefs about God, forms of liturgy, church organisation, religious education, charitable works (all very admirable but not the totality of what it means to be a Christian). So today there is a great thirst among church members for a deeper prayer life, for spiritual experience. This they are finding in the different methods of deep meditation. In a word, contemplative prayer is no longer regarded as the preserve of monks and nuns – those we call contemplatives – but it is the right of every Christian: a normal development of Christian prayer life.

Thirdly, meditation, whether regarded as a form of prayer or as an exercise in gaining deeper consciousness, is now considered as the chief means for humanity to bring about the New World Order, the Age of Aquarius, the Era of the Holy Spirit, or whatever name one likes to give the millennium ahead of us now that we see the structures (political, economic, social, religious) of our present twentieth-century culture collapsing all about us and desperately fighting a rearguard action to remain relevant.

And so we find ourselves in a transition stage regarding the place of meditation within the Christian Church. While some see it as a dangerous non-Christian practice emanating from eastern religions (the emptying-of-the-mind-and-allowing-a-legion-of-devils-to-enter syndrome) others see it as a Spirit-sent gift to restore the soul to church life.

Curiously, if sadly, the dynamic of the meditation movement within the Church is coming from the laity rather than the clergy. But perhaps this should not surprise us, for in the whole history of church life major changes have been initiated at the grassroots and not at the top of the hierarchical pyramid. What is sad, however, is that people are having to look outside their local Christian community to learn the art of meditation instead of finding it within their parish or congregation, the very place where they would expect to find the support of a meditating group.

24-7 Prayer

JAMES TOON

The experience of praying at length is changing people.

'Spring Harvest' is a large Christian event that takes place every year over the Easter holidays in the British seaside resorts of Minehead and Skegness. The programme includes worship, ministry, teaching, Bible study, lots of seminars, entertainment and much else besides.

This year I went to Spring Harvest for the first time. Of the many activities on offer, one stood out: a room set apart for prayer, twenty-four hours a day, seven days a week. I turned up at this shortly after midnight, one night towards the end of the week, to find a large, dimly-lit room, and about thirty mainly young people, some alone and some in small groups. Some were praying; others were gently singing; a few were painting or drawing, decorating the walls with art or poems in a creative expression of worship.

I found a place to sit down. This was a long way from the silence of the monthly Julian Meeting that I attend. But that didn't matter – the room was made holy by the continuous prayer of the preceding days. By the time I left, the sense of peace and the presence of God that filled the room had filled me too. I went back several times over the next couple of days and it was exactly the same.

Now if you take a large number of Christians and place them on the same site for a week, you might expect some of them at least to get together and pray, even after midnight. But this was no isolated event. In the past two years, about four hundred prayer rooms have operated, in some thirty countries across the world ranging from Australia to Zimbabwe, and in over one hundred locations in the UK alone. There are striking reports of answered prayer. Not only that, the experience of praying at length is changing people. It is becoming an addiction and a way of life. How has all this happened?

The idea of constant prayer is not new. The Bible enjoins it and the early Church practised it. There have been times of prolonged prayer down the centuries – most notably when a group of Moravians started to pray in a village near Dresden in August 1727 and maintained their prayer meeting for over a hundred years. In and beyond that period, over three thousand evangelists went out from the village to take the gospel to many countries, their most famous convert being John Wesley.

24–7 Prayer began by accident in September 1999 when a group of young people from Revelation Church in Chichester, in southern England, decided to pray continuously for a month in one-hour shifts. At the end they found they couldn't stop, so they kept going until Christmas. And the idea has spread rapidly across the UK and elsewhere since then. It seems easier to mobilise people to pray in this way, usually for a single concentrated week, sometimes longer, than through the more traditional weekly or monthly church prayer meeting. Although the focus is on youth, it is open to Christians of all ages.

24–7 Prayer would not have grown so quickly without the information and communication possibilities offered by the Internet. Their website, *www.24–7prayer.com,* includes articles on the principles of 24–7 prayer; a map and a diary showing where and when prayer rooms are operating; resources for starting and maintaining a prayer room; a gallery of art created inside prayer rooms; a 'wailing wall' to post prayer requests; and a series of on-line forums for debate and discussion, news about current prayer rooms, reports of answered prayer and so on.

Aside from the continual growth of prayer rooms, two new initiatives are emerging. The first is the establishment of 24–7 prayer teams to work alongside churches in locations outside the UK. These teams are not confined to prayer rooms but are engaging in a range of activities including prayer for local needs, mission, and practical help. Three teams are going out this summer, to Delhi, Ibiza and St Petersburg.

The second is the establishment of permanent prayer rooms – operating not just for a week or a month but for a whole year. Within the movement these are known as boiler rooms. This is obviously a significant undertaking. For it to happen anywhere it needs the support of several local churches, a suitable site, and, most importantly, enough people willing to sign up for prayer slots on a regular basis. At present, negotiations are underway for the establishment of boiler rooms in two cities in England. Such places could meet many needs – not least providing a prayer venue for Christians working in major cities who cannot find a church near them that is open during the week and reserved for prayer, not used for other activities.

What has 24–7 Prayer got to do with the Julian Meetings? On the face of it, not a great deal. The type of prayer is intercessory rather than contemplative; the average age of participants is much younger; the language used is different – passionate, modern, and radical, rather than gentle, quiet and mystical. But they do have this in common: both are fuelled by a longing for God and a desire to spend time – lots of time – in his company. Both recognise that prayer is the most important activity that can be undertaken and that it should be central to our way of life.

Something extraordinary has been started; and who knows where it will end?

In need of glasses? - a short story

LYNNE ROSAMOND

A decrepit old bus with curtains at its windows was parked in front of the smart office block. These travelling people were getting to be a real nuisance. The magazine I worked for had carried an article about them last week, so I knew all about their anti-social and scrounging ways. The police really ought to move them on from respectable areas like this; they really gave a very bad impression. I took a deep breath and braved the revolving doors of the office block, pleased to emerge on the inside, still looking reasonably dignified. I approached the receptionist who was touching up her bright red nails.

'Er, excuse me, I have an appointment with Mr J. Christ. I wonder if you could direct me to the right floor.'

Without looking up from her nails she mumbled something which I deciphered as 'Never heard of him, no one of that name here.'

'Oh no,' I thought. 'I've got the wrong address. Damn! What shall I do now? . . . Only one thing for it – find a phone and ring Mark at the office.' I turned and walked rapidly back to the dreaded revolving doors, gingerly stepping into them again. Just as I did so a smartly suited, distinguished-looking man with a briefcase (who, it occurred to me fleetingly, could be Mr Christ) stepped briskly into the doors on the other side and pushed them with such force that I was bumped with some violence from behind and shot out onto the pavement, heading with an unstoppable momentum towards the scratched red paint of the decrepit bus. I braced myself for impact. Then, quick as a flash, as if from nowhere, a man was between me and the bus. He clasped me tightly in his arms and I came to an abrupt halt.

'Oh, I'm so sorry,' I said, very embarrassed at the whole episode. But my gabbled explanation dwindled as I extricated myself from the man's arms and stepped back to get a clear look at my knight in shining armour – or rather, 'knight in scruffy denim'.

'That's quite all right; you're forgiven,' said my rescuer in a voice and with a look that would melt the heart of the most ardent of feminists. 'It's my pleasure,' he continued. 'You could have had a nasty bump on the side of my old jalopy.'

'Oh, it's *your* vehicle, is it?' I said, feeling a bit guilty at my previous uncharitable thoughts.

'Yes, vehicle and home too; I like to travel around. I meet lots of nice people that way – like yourself. Hey, you look quite shaken up. Come in and I'll brew you a cup of tea – make you feel better.'

It was an almost irresistible offer. But, just in time, I remembered I was supposed to be working, and if I didn't locate Mr Christ soon I would miss the chance of an important interview – essential in fact if I was going to come up with my article 'Is religion relevant today?' for next month's issue of the magazine. I thanked him, but declined his kind offer, briefly explaining the situation. As I turned to re-enter the office block in pursuit of the distinguished-looking man who I was now convinced must be Mr Christ, my rescuer said, 'He's not Mr Christ. I am, but you can call me Jesus. Come in, I've been expecting you. Now, how about that cup of tea?'

I stopped in my tracks, mouth open in disbelief. Then some of the stuff I had read in preparation for the interview flashed into my mind. This guy actually told people to identify with the poor and oppressed rather than the rich and powerful, to travel light, and to have their hearts set on giving love, not on getting wealth. It figured!

As I followed him up the steps into the old bus I could smell the lovely aroma of freshly baked bread, and when we reached the top of the steps I saw a variety of tasty looking loaves on the small work surface beside the little two ring calor gas cooker. 'Just called in at the bakers,' he said, seeing me look at the bread. 'Have a seat. I'll put the kettle on.' I sat down on a faded old settee that had been placed along one side of the bus. A huge vase of wild flowers – campion, buttercup, honeysuckle, dog rose – stood on a little table opposite, a blaze of colour against the white painted walls. Beside the small sink, near the cooker, stood a bottle of wine. I particularly noticed it because it was my favourite – claret. The interior of the bus was attractive in its simplicity and had the atmosphere of one who enjoyed life, not at all of the stern pleasure-hater which some of the followers of this man had led me to expect. I had to admit I was impressed: even if he didn't look much of a success, at least he did have the integrity to live the simple life that he taught others to embrace.

He handed me a mug of steaming tea and sat down opposite me, smiling. I smiled back, enjoying the moment. Then I remembered the questions I had prepared for the interview. Putting my tea carefully down beside the settee I took out my notebook and pencil.

'OK to ask you some questions then?' I asked with rather less of my usual assertiveness.

'Fire away,' he said cheerfully. So that's just what I did, asking his opinions on nuclear weapons, euthanasia, abortion, suffering, the oppression of blacks by whites, children by adults, women by men, the ignorant by the educated. His answers were earnest, thought-provoking, compassionate, often witty but never judgemental. But at one point he got really exasperated and exclaimed, 'What must I do to make people know really deep down how much God loves, accepts and forgives them? When they really know this they will be able to love each other more because they will fear less; they will be able to make sacrifices for one another, even die for one another.' When I commented (rather sarcastically I'm ashamed to say) that many of his followers found this part of his message very hard to accept, and even harder to put into practice, he merely smiled in a very solemn way as if he really did understand. 'It's not easy.' But then he brightened up and said that we could learn a lot about how to live from children. Part of me scoffed at the naivety of it. But then I looked at him and the way he was; and I – wondered.

During our interview I had gradually become aware that several 'people of the road' (to put it politely) had stopped by the open windows of the bus and were listening. They seemed fascinated. At last I got to the final question on my list: I asked him how he felt about the terrible things that were done by some of his followers in his name – wars, torture, oppression. During our time together he had shown many emotions – anger, sorrow, humour. But this was the first time he really lost his temper. It was alarming. 'My God!' he thundered, thumping the table so hard I thought it would turn right over. 'My God! Don't they have ears to hear or eyes to see? My message is clear enough. Love God, love yourself, love others as you love yourself!'

At that point the onlookers outside the bus shuffled off, alarmed by the vehemence of his anger. Jesus got up and walked over to the bottle of wine by the sink. 'Fancy a glass of wine before you go? It's very good, this claret, but I don't like drinking alone much; far rather have company. Are you hungry?' I was very much aware at that moment that I'd had no breakfast and it was way past lunch time. I nodded. 'We can share this bread. It's delicious – fresh this morning.' He laughed. 'I'll call the others back too.' He jumped out of the bus.

Five minutes later he and the vagrants sat passing round the wine –

he possessed only one glass – and tearing chunks of soft white bread from the loaves. They were thoroughly enjoying themselves. Jesus was telling them stories. 'Have you heard the one about the Tory MP and the vagrant who turned up for confession at the same time?' I heard him say. And then, 'How about the black punk-rocker who saved the life of a policeman who'd been shot by a gang robbing the NatWest bank – the punk had done a first-aid course while inside for beating up a cop!' How they all laughed. They loved it. They loved him.

Me – well, I felt out of it. I couldn't bring myself to share a glass with these people. It was disgusting, dangerous even. You never know what you might catch. Don't get me wrong though. I've nothing against giving them the odd copper now and then as I pass by. But drink from the same glass – ugh! I decided that Jesus, as he'd said himself, was not an easy leader to follow.

I crept quietly down the steps of the bus, hesitating as I reached the pavement. I had a strange feeling that I was turning away from something important, something unique. Or was it someone? My thoughts were brought to an abrupt end by my sudden awareness of odd looks from passers-by. I realized uncomfortably that I was emerging from a decrepit bus-load of laughing vagrants. I hurriedly turned away from the bus and set off up the road at a brisk pace, heading back to the office. I was excited about getting started on my article. I felt that this could be the one that could really mark a turning-point in my career. I quickened my pace, and as I reached the corner of the road I looked back for one last glimpse of the old bus. It had disappeared. The police must have finally moved him on. The road had regained its respectability, it was back to normal. I felt a pang of disappointment – the kind of feeling I'd had last Christmas when, on tearing open an interesting looking parcel from Aunt Mabel, I had discovered yet another pair of run–resistant tights! But then, as I looked back to where the old bus had been, I realised that things were not entirely back to normal. The vagrants who normally looked wretched, standing dejectedly by the wall hoping for donations, were now enthusiastically trying to give out chunks of bread to bemused passers-by. I could hardly believe my eyes. A great grin spread across my face. It was hilarious. I couldn't wait to write my article. A turning point. Definitely a turning point.

Dadirri

JAMES PATRICK

> *This is a spirituality of landscape: myths and memories . . . are written in rock and river and sand and plant.*

A visit to Australia today has to include Uluru (formerly Ayers Rock), that mysterious geographical phenomenon that is also an Aboriginal heritage site and shrine. It is situated symbolically right in the centre of the vast and empty hinterland. Each year, thousands of Australians from the coastal towns and cities make the journey to the interior to rediscover their national roots. For generations the 'dark' side of Australia has been rejected. Now the fractured national psyche is being healed as the country re-appropriates its own living tradition and ancient wisdom.

Here is a contemporary movement of the Spirit. The churches may not be the liveliest part of the Australian scene, but under the surface is a powerful spiritual surge. A people is hearing and responding to the call to 'come into the desert'.

The great crowds are – for the most part – silent, reverent, worshipful even, as they watch the massive rock turn rose-red in the light of dawn or sunset. The majority, in deference to Aboriginal susceptibilities, refrain from climbing. They listen attentively as the bush-ranger explains the significance in Aboriginal life of certain physical features. For this is a spirituality of landscape: myths and memories and what the Hebrews call 'Law' are written in rock and river and sand and plant. So what is called for is not detached observation but the seeing heart.

What draws so many visitors? In the 'neighbouring' town of Alice Springs – five hundred kilometres distant! – stands the Flynn Memorial United Church. Flynn of the outback, a Presbyterian minister, was the pioneer of the flying doctors. The builders' pious hopes that the church would become the Iona or Canterbury of Australia have not been realised in practice. Instead, Ayers Rock has become a centre of pilgrimage and the hope of national spiritual regeneration.

The Aborigines have something to give that modern Australia – and the rest of the developed world – needs desperately. A word from their own language group sums it up: *dadirri*, defined as contemplativeness or 'an inner deep listening and quiet still awareness' that makes us whole again.

But in turn Aboriginal mysticism can be seen as completed in Christian mysticism. According to Miriam-rose Ungunmerr, an Aboriginal Catholic writer, the ancient waiting and listening of her people has been answered by a new word from God.

This new word is Jesus . . .

Circle

KATE COMPSTON

Circle-sitting
like a bowl
we held the silence
shared the weight
between us
juggling, balancing
– until it seemed
quite effortless
and feather-light
– until the stillness
was the womb
that cradled us.

Later
the wisdom of the body
knew the moment and
not without pain
the contractions
pushed us away
from our connectedness.
Time to break circle
time to be born
into word and action.
But going with us
stillness within

to make the ordinary shine.
The waters that break
are not lost. They
will be taken up, our days
nourished by them.
They will fall
gentle as rain
again, again . . .

Acknowledgements

Our thanks to the following for permission to reprint:

Ave Maria Press for Joyce Rupp's poem 'Astonished'. Excerpted from *Out of the Ordinary: Prayers, Poems, and Reflections for Every Season* by Joyce Rupp OSM. Copyright © 2000 by Ave Maria Press, PO Box 428, Notre Dame, IN 46556, www.avemariapress.com. Used with permission of the publisher.

Canterbury Press for 'Circle' by Kate Compston from *Seeing Christ in Others* (ed. G. Duncan).

Church Times for 'When the Children Want to Stop' by Julie McGuiness, which first appeared in the *Church Times Educational Supplement.*

Darton, Longman and Todd Ltd for 'Sinking into Silence' by Margaret Silf from *Taste and See*; for 'Playfulness and Prayer' by Wanda Nash from *Come, Let Us Play!*; and for 'The Meaning of Things' by Basil Hume from *The Mystery of the Incarnation.*

Faber & Faber, for the quotation on page 160 from stanza 5 of T.S. Eliot's poem 'The Dry Salvages'.

The *Christian Parapsychologist* for 'The Spiritual and the Psychic' by Robert Llewelyn.

The Community of the Holy Cross for 'The Joy and Strength of Union: Thomas Traherne and God's holy days'. It comes from a series of Spirituality leaflets published free of charge by the Community at Rempstone Hall, Loughborough, LE12 6RG.

The Guild of St Raphael for 'Being Honest with God' by Angela Ashwin, from their journal *Chrism* (Original title: 'Sometimes Prayer is Bleeding').

The Leprosy Mission, for 'Being – and Doing' by Eddie Askew from 'No Strange Land'.

The Methodist Publishing House for 'Celtic Knot' by Ann Lewin © from *Flashes of Brightness.*

The Society of St John Evangelist newsletter for 'Trailing Clouds of Glory' by Jenny Moulton.

The Tablet for 'My Glimpse of Death' by Martin Israel, and 'Light from a Mystic' by Robert Llewelyn; also the report of the Julian Meetings' twenty-first anniversary retreat which appeared in *The Tablet* under the title 'Without Words'.

Trethewey Press (3 Dornfield Rd, Ipplepen, Newton Abbott, Devon TQ12 5SH) for all poems by Joy French.

Harry Williams for lines from his book *Tensions* (Mitchell Beazley, 1976) which are quoted in Wanda Nash's *Playfulness and Prayer.*

All the authors of the articles and poems in this collection.

All those who have edited the *Julian Meetings Magazine* in the period covered by this book: Pamela Fawcett, Graham Johnson, Deidre Morris and James Toon.

About the contributors

The editor has tried to contact the writers of all the pieces selected from past issues of the JM Magazine, *to ask for their permission to reprint and for a biographical note. Where this has not been possible the name is omitted, but the editor would be glad to hear from them. Her email address is wakeman@iolfree.ie.*

Angela Ashwin is a speaker and writer on prayer and spirituality. Her books include *Heaven in Ordinary, The Book of a Thousand Prayers, Wait and See,* and *Wait and Trust;* also a flexible daily office, *Woven into Prayer.* Her newest book is called *The Wine Danced.* She is now on the Church of England's Liturgical Commission.

Eddie Askew with his wife Barbara worked in India for fifteen years with The Leprosy Mission and later became its International Director. Now retired, he concentrates on his writing and painting and is a best-selling Christian author. They live in a Nottinghamshire village with their dog Cromwell.

Nanette Bailey is a member of the committee of the East Midlands SPIDIR spiritual direction team. She gives individual spiritual direction, including taking people through the Ignatian 19th Annotation.

Gail Ballinger is an Anglican with a Methodist background. She is married to a priest and is a member of the Julian Meetings' Advisory Group.

Ivy Bishop is an active member of the local Anglican churches, the Julian Meetings, the Mothers' Union and the Focolare Movement.

Mary Blake has been published in a number of small presses both in Ireland and in England, and in anthologies. She has won various competitions, is a member of the Ver Poets – and also of the Julian Meetings in Little Gaddesden, Hertfordshire.

Hilary Burn is a lay preacher in the United Reformed Church. She was a member of the Julian Meetings' Advisory Group from 1976 to 1993.

Glen Cavaliero is a member of the Faculty of English in Cambridge. He has published half a dozen critical studies, including *The Supernatural and English Fiction* (Oxford, 1995); and four books of poems.

'A CHC Sister': Sister Mary Michael CHC is a member of the Anglican Religious Community of the Holy Cross and seeks to live a life of prayer according to the Benedictine monastic tradition.

Sandy Chubb was a yoga teacher and is now the Director of The Prison Phoenix Trust (PO Box 328, Oxford OX2 7HF).

Kate Compston is a Quaker attender as well as a 'continuing if very questioning' member of the United Reformed Church, of which she is an ordained minister. She leads retreats and Quiet Days, and works as a psychodynamic counsellor. She has contributed poems and prayers to many books, and edited the URC's *Textures of Tomorrow.*

David Conner was Vicar of Great St Mary's, the University Church of Cambridge, from 1987 to 1994, and then Bishop of Lynn in the Diocese of Norwich. Since 1998 he has been Dean of Windsor and is also now Bishop to the Forces.

Jim Cotter is a free-range vicar whose wordsmithy produces books, articles, talks, and sermons. He publishes as Cairns Publications and takes care of a church in North Wales as a 'small pilgrim place'.

Meister Eckhart was a German mystic, teacher and preacher (1260–1327).

Chris Eyden, formerly an actor in theatre and television, is now a parish priest. As Vicar of St Mark's, Wimbledon, he also conducts retreats.

Joy French became a Christian in 1960, and from the 1970s onwards has led retreats, Quiet Days and prayer workshops. She lives in Devon and has produced three books of poems, *Notes and Queries, Second Thoughts* and *Terce.*

Simon Goodrich at the time of writing this article lived at The Anchorhold in Sussex, a place of exploration into contemplative prayer begun by Herbert Slade SSJE

Christopher Gregorowski is Bishop of the Table Bay region in Cape Town, South Africa. He recently conducted an Annual Quiet Day for JM-South Africa, including this address.

Tony Hawes is now fit and well. He is retired and lives with his wife in the quiet town of Reepham in Norfolk. In recent summers he has held monthly Quiet Days in his 'small but beautiful' garden.

John Hawkins is an architect, but was ordained at the age of sixty-two, and now pursues a retirement ministry focused on creative arts retreats, spiritual direction and healing. He was a member of the Julian Meetings' Advisory Group for some years.

Martin Heyns is a minister of the Dutch Reformed Church in South Africa. Having been in ministry for twenty-nine years, he finds close ecumenical relationships a necessity in the process of moving away from a one-sided rationalist experience of God.

Mary Holliday was one of the first Methodist women in England to be ordained. Among many activities she was involved in the National Centre for Christian Communities and Networks (NACCAN), the Methodist Retreat Group, the Association for Promoting Retreats, and the National Retreat Centre. She served for several years on the JM Advisory Group.

Basil Hume was the Roman Catholic Cardinal Archbishop of Westminster until his death in 1999.

Martin Israel started his career as a pathologist and became an Anglican priest in 1975. He has written a number of books including *Summons to Life, Precarious Living, The Pain that Heals*, and most recently *Learning to Love.*

Graham Johnson is an Anglican priest, Chaplain and Inter-faith Advisor to the Bishop of Leicester, and a member of the Julian Meetings' Advisory Group.

Andrew Lane is the Superior of the Society of St Luke, an Anglican religious community dedicated to care and prayer for the suffering and their carers.

Ann Lewin is a former teacher, now a writer and retreat/Quiet Day leader. Her books include *Candles and Kingfishers* and *Flashes of Brightness.*

Robert Llewelyn, formerly Chaplain at the Julian Shrine in Norwich, is general editor of the highly acclaimed *Enfolded in Love* series (DLT) and author of many other books. He has been awarded the Cross of St Augustine by the Archbishop of Canterbury.

Julie McGuiness is a part-time counsellor, part-time freelance writer and qualified Myers-Briggs practitioner. She is also an Anglican Reader, and is based in Cheshire.

Sister Margaret Magdalen CSMV is at present the Sister Provincial of the Community of St Mary the Virgin in South Africa, and is heading up the Spirituality Commission in the diocese there, where she teaches, preaches, conducts retreats. In her early years she was a Baptist missionary. She has written a great number of books, including *Transformed by Love, The Hidden Face of Jesus,* and *Furnace of the Heart* (all published by Darton, Longman & Todd Ltd).

Deidre Morris describes herself as an ecumenical Anglican; a wife, mother and friend; gardener, cook and lacemaker; realist and dreamer.

Jenny Moulton has done 'a bit of teaching and a bit of counselling', but says her main career has been as homemaker, mother and now grandmother.

Barbara Muir spent most of her working life with oil exploration companies in Nigeria and Turkey. Returning to the UK she married a priest, and now as a widow lives in Norwich, with a busy life centering on the Cathedral.

Wanda Nash, one of the earliest members of Julian Meetings, started writing about the use of silence nearly twenty years ago. She leads retreats, sometimes with her husband who is an Archeacon Emeritus, though these have to fit in between enjoying her four daughters and eight grandchildren.

Rachel Noel is twenty-six and is employed as a project manager. In her local parish church near Southampton she is involved in the youth work, the music and making banners.

James Patrick studied Arts and Divinity at Glasgow, Edinburgh and Oxford. He is the Minister of the Gardens Presbyterian Church, Cape Town, and currently National Convenor of the Julian Meetings in South Africa.

Brother Ramon was a Franciscan, and author of several books. At the time of his death in June 2000 he was a member of the Glasshampton community.

Ann Richards is a member of the Julian Meetings' Advisory Group. She lives in south-east London and teaches mathematics to adults.

Lynn Roper is the contact for a Julian Meeting in Luton. From agnosticism she became a Christian after the birth of her first child and, when ill-health made it impossible for her to go to church, found a spiritual lifeline in JM.

Gill Russell lives in Leicester. An 'early' Julian and, approaching retirement, she is exploring oblature of a contemplative community. She was at one time Executive Officer of the Retreat Association and editor of *The Vision*. She has also worked at Launde Abbey.

Sarah Salisbury is a wife and mother, part-time school administrator and part-time student at Southampton University. She is involved in leading worship and youth work at her local church.

Nicola Slee is a freelance writer and lecturer based at the Queen's Foundation, Birmingham. She has written poetry since childhood, and has had a number of poems published in journals and anthologies.

Jenny Smeed works as a checkout operator in her local supermarket, and sings in her church choir. She has had over forty poems published. Two of these were shortlisted for the 'Top 100 Poets' award by Forward Press, one of which was 'Reflections'.

Adrian B. Smith is a member of the Missionaries of Africa Society. Ordained a Catholic priest in 1955, he has spent much of his life in Africa. He has an MA in ecumenical theology and has been active in several organisations working for change in the Church and in the world. He is the author of many books, including *A Key to the Kingdom of Heaven* on Transcendental Meditation and *A New Framework for Christian Belief.*

Don Stephen was for some years the National Convenor for the Julian Meetings in South Africa. He is an Associate of the Benedictine Holy Cross Order.

Ena Taylor was 'a Norfolk girl' and, with her husband, farmed in the Midlands until 1966 when they moved to Australia. In 1986 she graduated in Comparative Literature and now belongs to a writing group in the Perth area.

Doreen Thurston and her family have lived in Tasmania, Papua New Guinea and the Solomon Islands. After several bereavements she is now living in England, with the love and support of her remaining family and her church family.

Michael Tiley is an Anglican, married to a Roman Catholic from Mexico. They have two daughters and share an ecumenical home in London.

James Toon has been Editor of the *Julian Meetings Magazine* since 2000, and is a member of the Advisory Group. He is an Anglican layman.

Liz Tyndall became a member of the Julian Meetings' Advisory Group in its early days, and stayed on it for twenty years. She became an Anglican priest and is still working in retirement.

Henry van Dyke hymn writer, 1852–1933.

Hilary Wakeman is a priest in the Church of Ireland and a Canon Emeritus of Norwich Cathedral. As a laywoman, she was the accidental founder of the Julian Meetings.

Yvonne Walker is the UK Co-ordinator of the Julian Meetings. and chairs the Methodist Retreat Group.

Fiona Wallace has two children and a very busy husband. She works one day a week with adults with learning difficulties, and is a member of the Julian Meetings' Advisory Group.

Hebe Welbourn has been Warden of the ecumenical Elsie Brigg's House of Prayer in Bristol since 1991. She is an Anglican and goes to an inner-city church on Sundays but also attends Friends' meetings when she can and is a member of a Zen Buddhist group in Bristol.

Jim Wellington is a priest in the Church of England and a member of its General Synod. He has a particular interest in Orthodox spirituality and has been on pilgrimage to Mount Athos as part of a sabbatical study of the history and practice of the Jesus Prayer.

Index